A YEAR OF CREATIVE
WRITING
PROMPTS
II

LOVE IN INK

The writing prompts contained in this book are meant to inspire writers to create. Each prompt was imagined and recorded by a member of the *Love in Ink* team. Any resemblance to writing prompts or stories already in existence and circulation is accidental.

Write on! ☺

ISBN-13: 978-1794317840
ISBN-10: 1794317848

INDEX

INTRODUCTION

A Year of Creative Writing Prompts is a series meant to inspire writers and kick writer's block to the curb! Volume I helps authors establish good writing habits through a regime of daily writing prompts. Volume II reaffirms those habits by providing a plethora of ideas for many hours of happy writing.

In this book, you will find over 1000 prompts in 20+ genres. That's more than three prompts per day, every day, for an entire year! There is something for everyone inside. Grab a pen; your story is waiting!

Write on ☺

Love in Ink

 CTION/ADVENTURE

Action and Adventure go hand in hand. Stories in this genre should be exciting, quick-paced, and packed with action - and so are the prompts below!

☐ Jason Rowe is a proud member of the top 1%. A business trip to Eastern Europe has Rowe re-evaluating his outlook on life, courtesy of his traitorous son-in-law.

Rowe survives a violent assault via an unplanned dive into a swift river. The thugs his son-in-law had hired leave him for dead. Rowe isn't far from it when he pulls himself ashore. He is disorientated, bloody, and absolutely lost. That doesn't stop him from making his way back home.

☐ A young girl hides in a boarded-up house during a game of hide-and-seek. The house isn't empty. The girl sees something she really, really shouldn't have seen. She has to sneak out before the bad people find her.

☐   Write a chase scene. A man is running from a group of tough-looking guys. Make the action twisty, both in terms of the terrain (an inner-city concrete jungle, a forest, a mountainous region) and the man's motivation. Make him the villain, not the victim, but keep this particular twist of the story hidden until the very end.

☐   A woman is on her way to work. She is running very late, on a day her company is holding a high-level meeting. The woman is in such a hurry that she misses the dead man manning the security booth in the lobby. She slips in an elevator just as the doors are closing. The man inside gives her a pause. He looks like every hired gun Hollywood has ever depicted. The floor the man has selected is the one that hosts the woman's company. She tries to think.

Eight floors to figure out a plan of action.

☐   A thief sneaks into a mansion with the purpose of making off with as much as he can. He doesn't count on catching another crime in progress - a much more gruesome offense than mere theft. The thief ends up fleeing the house with the owner's young child, now an orphan. Bad, bad men are after them both.

☐ A pizza place takes down the order of a repeat customer. The man taking the order hears something strange on the other end of the line. The call cuts, but not before someone - someone definitely *not* the customer - says, "you've got ten minutes before I shoot you full of lead."

The pizzeria worker is an ex-cop. He calls the police - on his way to the customer's house. He's got a car, training, and the need to *do* something when he knows someone else's in trouble.

The clock is ticking...

☐ Ed's father has the habit of dragging him along on business trips, ostensibly to "widen Ed's horizons." Ed would much prefer to be spending his Easter break at home, playing with his friends. Instead, he is stuck "widening his horizons" in a hotel half a world from everyone he knows.

Ed decides enough is enough, and sneaks out to explore the tiny city. He finds an unexpected partner in crime in a local boy. Write of their silly adventures. Bonus points if Ed doesn't speak the local language, and his new friend doesn't speak English.

☐ An aging warrior makes his way to a large city, home to a powerful King. He is chasing after whispers of a woman he loved, now rumored to live in the city with a child of an age that would make it the warrior's own.

The warrior finds his old love dead, and the child gone, as if it had never been. There are plenty of whispers and hired men scuttling about in the shadows. The warrior is certain his child is still in the city. Figuring out where would involve uncovering the unlikely history of his lost lover.

☐ The King of a vast, powerful kingdom, is on his deathbed. The Crown Prince(ss) is nowhere to be found.

The young noble wants nothing to do with ruling the nation. The next person in line for the throne is unsuitable, to say the least (and evil. So very, very evil). The Captain of the Knights is tasked with finding the errant royal and dragging him/her back to the castle to be crowned. The Captain in turn hires help in the form of a mercenary with whom he's had dealings in the past. The two search the land for their ruler-to-be as the clock ticks down on the King's life.

☐   Saving the neighbor's cat from getting run over by a car shouldn't lead to getting indoctrinated into the Italian mafia. *Shouldn't* being the operative word.

☐   A homeless man becomes witness to a brutal kidnapping. He knows that the police won't find the victim in time - the men who had taken him/her aren't looking for ransom. They're settling a grudge.

☐   An online friend "goes dark" - that is, they disappear from their usual online platforms without notice. Your character can't help but feel something has happened to them. They figure out the person's general location and seek them out, across the country, without knowing as much as their name.

☐   A construction worker finds a child wandering around his work site. The girl is lost, has no shoes on, and is too scared to speak. The man takes it upon himself to find her parents. He manages to learn a few details from the girl and his own observations - he used to be a detective, before a bad case took his partner and his love for the job. It soon becomes obvious to him that the girl is no random child. There are people after her; dangerous people. Something about her is looking familiar, as well...

☐   A traveling circus visits a small town. The kids are ecstatic, and the parents are having a wonderful time out among bright booths and fun rides.

That is, until a child disappears without a trace. The child's parents are frantic, and the circus owners are eager to hush the whole thing and find the child before alerting the local police becomes necessary. The circus itself isn't large - someone must have seen something.

Clues piece together one by one, pointing to where the child has gone. Build the story around these clues, making sure to keep up a feeling of excitement, color, and all things circus.

☐   A woman with incredibly bad luck hires a bodyguard to help her survive the million mishaps she is subjected to on a daily basis. The man thinks her mad, but doesn't question an easy gig. He quickly finds himself struggling to keep the woman from danger, which seems to lurk anywhere the woman passes.

☐   A man is house-sitting for his best friend. He manages to lose her cat within an hour of setting foot in the apartment. The friend is coming home in two days; the man has a cat to find, and his tracks to cover.

☐   Start a story halfway through a quest, with the hero and his/her entourage already well into their journey. Their objective is within reach, but the enemy has not yet been faced and defeated. Then, the unthinkable happens - the hero dies. The secondary character has to step up and fill the hero's shoes.

☐   A con-man on the run from the law lies his way into a travelling band of warriors. He manages to evade the soldiers after him, but finds himself involved in a much more dangerous and difficult quest.

☐   A retired swordsman is pulled into a job as a favor to a friend. The man is hired to guard the son of a local nobility as the brat journeys to the capital, for some grand shin-ding or another. The swordsman finds the whole thing a waste of time (on his part) and coin (on that of the kid's father). There are plenty of men guarding the convoy already. Surely, they don't need him?

The swordsman is proven wrong when the convoy is attacked - by the very men hired to protect it. He makes it out with the boy he's supposed to guard, but they are a long way from home and safety.

☐   A mysterious traveler passes through a village. He is not a stranger, but the people of the village have long forgotten him.

He hasn't forgotten them. A purpose carries him to his birthplace, and his stay there will be eventful, to say the least.

☐   A dangerous man and a federal agent play a cat-and-mouse game in a busy office building in the heart of a major city. The agent is trying to keep a low profile, aware that if he presses too hard, the man he is chasing will go for broke and hurt innocent bystanders. The criminal in question is aware that he is being chased, and amused enough to keep playing the game.

☐   Your character wakes up in an unfamiliar house. The place is deserted - there is no furniture or pictures on the wall, and cobwebs and dust cover everything. A thick forest surrounds the property on all sides.

How did your character get there? Do they find their way back home?

☐   A man is waiting for his friend. The friend shows up two hours late, with the most outlandish excuse.

Challenge: make this a dialogue-only story.

☐ A young child wanders away from his/her parents during a vacation in a foreign city, and quickly loses his/her way in the unfamiliar surroundings. Instead of getting scared, the child approaches the challenge of finding his/her family as an adventure.

☐ A puppy strays a little too far away from home. Write about the puppy's adventure trying to get back to their humans! Introduce both helpful and devious animal characters who help or hinder the puppy's quest.

☐ A man with a boring office job goes adventuring every weekend. He picks a direction and drives, going wherever the road takes him. If he meets people who need help, he helps them. Most often, he simply enjoys life and his own company.

☐ Who doesn't love a story featuring a giant creature of some kind? Write such a tale, but with a twist: the giant critter wrecking havoc in your metropolis must be an animal most would see as adorable and harmless.

How would a bunny conquer New York? What sort of destruction can a hamster wreck in Tokyo?

☐   A parent forgets to pick up their child after school. Cue them racing through traffic to get to their son/daughter, in a panic of guilt and sheer disbelief they had done such a thing.

Focus on the journey and the parent's mental state. Have the story end with the child happily playing with their teacher, totally unaware anything had been amiss.

☐   A small flower shop has been struggling to make ends meet. When a customer requests an extraordinarily large order, the owners are thrilled - until they realize the order is express-delivery, scheduled for that very same day! Hectic flower arrangements, scrambling to find extra drivers, and pulling disgruntled teenagers in to help the family business ensue.

☐   Two boys are telling scary stories inside a tent, in the middle of the night. Meanwhile, a bear is prowling around their campsite and the boys' parents are frantically trying to think of ways to get the animal to leave.

☐   A woman sneaks away from her company's hotel during a business trip, foregoing networking events and the general schmoozing her colleagues are indulging. She explores the countryside instead, letting her inner child play.

☐   Linda has recently retired from her job of forty years. She finds herself at loose ends, with nothing to do all day but watch soaps and get angry at the news.

That is, until a fairy pops in for tea, bearing an offer of great adventure.

Note: If fantasy is not your cup of tea, feel free to substitute "fairy" with a relative or friend in need of Linda's aid in an unlikely task.

☐   A diplomatic envoy is attacked during a visit to a friendly nation. Several high-level diplomats are taken hostage. One among them has military background. Another excels at strategy. The two conspire to free themselves and the rest of the group from their abductors.

☐   A man falls into an underground cave while hiking. He twists his ankle, but is otherwise unharmed. The cave itself is deep underground. A cramped passageway leads somewhere, perhaps deeper underground, perhaps to a way out. The man must decide whether to take this dark passage, or attempt climbing up on his bad ankle.

☐   Miranda has the most boring job ever. She spends her workday imagining herself taking part in ridiculous adventures - until the day something strange crashes through the window next to Miranda's cubicle.

☐   Sam has lived his whole life in an isolated community with a cult-like society. He has sought means of escape ever since his mother died, and he witnessed the real cruelty of the community's leaders.

The world beyond the town's gates is described as uninhabitable and dangerous. Sam has no reason to trust anything he has learned growing up, but lack of knowledge means he doesn't know what to expect upon leaving the compound. He takes the risk nonetheless.

☐   Two neighboring apartments once used to belong to a single family. As such, the apartments share a door. Hidden behind heavy furniture on both sides, the door is not discovered until the young children whose bedrooms it connects stumble upon it. The kids make the door their secret, and grow up playing with each other as if they were siblings. They share games and adventures, with their respective parents none the wiser.

☐ A storm brings a dangerous stranger to a man's door. The man decides to let the stranger in. He is unaware of the person's identity, but instincts soon tell him he may have made a mistake and must now tread carefully.

☐ Climbing trees is fun. Getting down once you reach the top... Steve may not have thought this through.

☐ A train is derailed in the middle of a forest. There are no means of communication, and the train's absence won't be noticed until the following morning. Passengers and crew bunker down for the night, telling stories to pass the time.

A few entrepreneurial souls find an opportunity in the accident. Three crimes are being planned: a theft, a con, and a murder. Weave the three together, with the criminals going after one another without realizing that their victims hold an ill intent of their own.

☐ A thief pickpockets an undercover cop who has just blown his cover. The cop notices. So do the men who are chasing after the cop. Thief and policeman are forced to flee together, each none too happy about the other's presence.

Focus the story on the chase and the interaction between the thief and the cop.

☐   A lost phone sets off a chain of events that begin with a missed phone call and end with the story's protagonist facing off the Russian mafia.

Fill the sequence in between.

☐   Two strangers share a cab during a stormy night, and fall for each other over the course of the ride. They exchange contact information. Bad luck has both losing the other's details. The two are nonetheless determined to find each other. Cue a game of seek spanning a metropolitan city, with the two at times missing one another by seconds.

☐   Write a story from the point of view of a someone who has just moved to a new city. The person jogs in the morning . On their very first run, they stumble onto a dead body - as joggers are wont to do.

Your character is unfortunate enough to find the killer along with the corpse. Their morning jog turns into a full-on sprint through an unfamiliar town, with the killer hot on their heels.

☐   An outgoing, happy person is determined to befriend their broody neighbor. Style the story as an adventure, with the neighbor doing their best to fend off the protagonist's increasingly excessive attempts at friendship.

☐ A woman accidentally drills a hole through her wall into the neighboring apartment while trying to hang a painting. She doesn't think much of it; the painting covers the hole on her side, and some sort of furniture blocks it off on her neighbor's. The noise bleed-through has gone up, but not enough to bother her.

Until she overhears a phone call she really, really shouldn't have.

☐ A family's dog keeps wandering off during the day for hours at a time, only to return dirty and tired. The family ties a camera to their pet's collar, and make an astonishing discovery: Their dog is a real-life hero, spending its days helping people and animals in need.

☐ Sam's face is much too expressive, in a manner that makes the man appear quite scary. Unfortunate genetics routinely land Sam in strange situations. The latest? A polite smile offered in passing somehow results in Sam's earning the respect of a hitman.

☐ Three brothers swear to avenge the murder of their father. One of them finds his resolve shaken when the motives of the killer come to light.

☐ A woman is kidnapped. She manages to untie herself and attack her kidnapper, taking him/her by surprise. They are in a car. The kidnapper loses control of the wheel in the struggle, leading to a nasty crash. The kidnapper is rendered unconscious. The woman finds herself in the middle of a dark forest, with no way to orient herself. She must find a way out before the kidnapper regains consciousness.

☐ Alexei is a great reader of character. He is able to find the right person for whatever he needs done, wherever he happens to be - a skill that serves him well, as an internationally-wanted con-artist.

☐ During a heist, a man forced into a life of crime in order to provide for his family encounters someone who has never experienced hardship. The man decides to save this stranger's life, despite the fact that doing so will result in the heist failing and land him in serious trouble.

HILDREN'S FICTION

Tales in this genre should appeal to young readers, serving as a source of knowledge and entertainment. The prompts below vary in subject matter, ranging from sweet stories for the youngest of readers to more serious topics meant for older children. Write with joy in your heart!

☐ A little girl falls asleep with her favorite storybook open on her bed. She wakes up in the world of the book. Reaching the end will allow her to return home. If only she could remember how the story ends!

☐ Tell a story about a young boy/girl that emigrates to a foreign country with his/her parents. Center the story around the child and their experiences.

☐ A little girl loses something during playtime at kindergarten. She starts crying. Her classmates take it upon themselves to find their friend's most important thing.

☐   A child decides to help their mom/dad with chores. They mess up, but it's the thought that counts!

☐   A young boy/girl saves a tiny animal from a downpour. They become fast friends, much to the chagrin of the child's babysitter.

☐   Write a short, Aesop-style story, teaching a child something of value. The story's characters should be animals, as befitting of the genre.

☐   A young child tells their parent/older sibling about their day. Make the tale outlandish and imaginative!

☐   Write a story explaining a difficult - but not necessarily upsetting - concept to a child.

☐   A day at the zoo turns into a detective show when Zoey loses her pet hamster. Zoey and her brother must find the poor creature before it disappears into the city, or wanders into the wrong cage.

☐   First day of school for a group of anxious, overexcited first-graders begins with tears and ends in giggles and many new friendships. And a dug-up school garden (and worms in pockets).

☐   Allie tells everyone she is a fairy princess - her parents, her teachers, even Ralph, the family's pet dog. No one believes her. Well, except Ralph - and the fairies living in her mother's garden.

☐   Write two short tales about bullying, aimed at young readers. One of the stories should be from the perspective of a child being bullied, and teach one what should be done to deal with a bully. The other story should be from the bully's perspective, and convey a message of acceptance and encouragement to do better rather than berate about the wrongs of bullying. Both stories must feature characters around the age of the story's audience (younger children).

☐   Write an experience from your own life in a style fit for a children's fairy tale. You can make characters into supernatural creatures - make your first boss an ogre, your ex - a dragon... Generally have fun with the story, and make it fun to read!

☐ Nelly lost her sock. Now her favorite pair is incomplete! It's dark out, time for bed. Nelly's mother had promised they would look for the sock together in the morning, but Nelly can't sleep not knowing its fate. She slips out of bed and braves the dark, scary places in her room - under the bed, in the closet, behind the dresser - in her quest for the missing sock.

☐ A young child pleads the case for having a puppy. Make the argument logical - in child's terms.

☐ A family goes to the zoo with their young child for the first time. Tell a story of the experience, from the child's perspective.

☐ Being different often means being lonely. A little girl is shunned at school for something she can't help. She is too kind to hold grudges; she acts friendly, even with the meanest of her classmates.

Optional: Fast forward ten years, and the little lonely girl has grown up into a kind, confident young woman with true friends of the kind that usually exist only in books.

☐   Young children are a little bit magic. They can talk with animals, and see spirits and godly beings. Too bad adults think a child is just being silly when they talk about the dragon they met in the garden...

☐   Tell a story in which the protagonist makes a mistake or is otherwise not right about something they passionately insist to be true. The moral should be that people can be wrong, and that being wrong is okay as long as one learns from a mistake and tries to put things to right.

☐   Write a story featuring two kindergartners on their very first day of school. They react very differently to being away from home. Have the each child's personality shine through in their behavior.

☐   Kids are very intuitive, and understand more of the world than adults believe. Write a story in which the child protagonist sees through a situation better than the adults around them, and surprises everyone with their insight at the very end of the tale.

☐   A child wanders away from his/her family during an outing. Write the story from the child's point of view.

☐   Two siblings are visiting their grandmother. The grandmother lives in a small village, while the children's parents have made their home in a nearby city. The siblings play in the countryside, make friends with the local kids, and generally have a grand time.

☐   A little boy has his very first birthday party. He is a little overwhelmed by all the chaos, and ends up liking the quiet time he spends with his parents after the party more.

☐   Children see the extraordinary in everyday situations. Write a story about a young child riding on a bus for the first time. The child's reaction to the bus and passing scenery reminds the adults around him/her about what is truly important in life.

☐   Tell a story set on Halloween, from the perspective of a child who has gone trick-or-treating with friends but would really prefer to be home, tucked safely away on this most scary holiday.

☐   Your protagonist breaks a rule at home, and must face the consequences.

☐ Your protagonists faces all kinds of childhood fears - the monster under the bed, thunder rattling the windows in the dead of night, that one creepy tree that looks like a goblin in the dark - and emerges victorious by making up silly stories about them.

☐ A family is celebrating the first birthday of a baby girl. Her three-year-old brother takes the festivities and his responsibility as an older brother very seriously, to the amusement of his parents.

☐ A class goes on a field trip to an old, historic town. Focus on a few of the children; what does each one wish to see? To buy? Is anyone buying gifts for their family, or candy for themselves?

☐ A bunny and a wolf cub share a shelter during an unexpected storm. The bunny is old and wise, and teaches the wolf cub a thing or two while rain pelts away outside.

☐ A kindergarten puts on a play. The teacher lets the children pick their roles, and ends up with a boy playing the princess and a girl filling in for the brave knight.

☐   A bear cub teams up with a fox kit to steal honey from a human farm. The two end up befriending a human child, and have a wonderful time playing together.

☐   Write a short story featuring a child superhero. What kind of powers do they have? How do they use them?

☐   Make up a silly song a parent might sing to their child in order to teach them something, or persuade them to do a chore.

☐   A witch curses a small town, turning the townsfolk into animal equivalents of their previous selves. The only person not affected by the curse is a young child, who must now find a way to break the spell.

☐   Retell your favorite book as a story meant for children. Condense the plot into a short tale that would be understood by young readers, without taking away from the book's overall message.

☐   Was there something with which you struggled as a child? Write a story around a topic you found difficult or confusing when you were young, in a way that would help children deal with the same issue.

☐ A child befriends the shy, quiet new kid in their class. The two bond by getting into trouble together.

☐ A young girl is traveling with her parents. It is her first time on a train, and she is excited by everything. Walk the reader through the train through this girl's eyes. You can set the story in modern times, or a time when traveling by train was a great marvel.

☐ Two brothers catch a frog while playing near a small stream. They take it back home, to show to their mother. Only the frog doesn't exactly stay put, and the show-and-tell turns into a merry chase around the house.

☐ What piece of childhood magic did you hold onto the longest? Santa Claus? The Easter Bunny? The Tooth Fairy? Write a story about the particular character or belief, describing it in the manner you used to perceive it as a child.

☐ Leah finds a stray kitten. She knows that she can't keep it, but is determined to find a good home for her new friend.

☐   Cathy keeps an album filled with pictures of her favorite people, places, and things. She writes short paragraphs under each photo that goes into the album, explaining why it is important to her. Write ten of these short paragraphs.

Note: Cathy is eight years old. Build a realistic collection of pictures she would have chosen to keep, and mind the wording of the descriptions so they fit her age and a particular character.

☐   An owl makes a nest in a tree facing the window of a young boy. The boy is initially scared of the owl and its late-night hooting. He makes up a story featuring the bird in order to overcome his fear. Write that story.

☐   Dan is on his first sleepover at a friend's house. He wakes from a nightmare late at night, and grows even more frightened when he realizes his parents aren't there. Dan's friend helps him chase the bad dreams away.

☐   Tara keeps a plant as a pet. She loves it as much as any child does the family cat or dog, and takes good care of her green friend.

☐   A household pet tells of life with its best friend - the family's young child.

☐ Galia's family celebrates the winter holidays by exchanging hand-made gifts. Galia is finally old enough to make her own presents, and is excited to give something she has created to her loved ones.

☐ A city kid goes on a trip to the countryside, and spends a weekend discovering the beautiful surroundings with the local kids.

☐ A powerful storm disrupts the internet connection of an entire neighborhood, forcing kids to do the unthinkable - play outside. Older kids teach younger ones the classics, games they themselves had not played in years. By the time the internet comes back on, most children are no longer interested in pixels; they are much happier playing with their new friends.

☐ A child really, really wants to play a specific instrument. They have no natural talent. Their parents are not musicians, and can offer little guidance. The child makes up for lack of such advantages with hard work, and is eventually able to play beautifully.

OMEDY

Comedy and Tragedy are two faces of the same coin. Both involve high stakes and drama; unlike tragedies, however, comedic tales always, always end well. Delight your readers and add some laughter to the world with the prompts below!

☐   Sam is having the worst day in his life. Everything that can go wrong does, in a spectacular fashion.

Write a day of ridiculous bad luck. Bonus points: Make the saying, "everything happens for a reason" true, and turn Sam's misfortune into something amazing.

☐   A young man breaks into the home of an elderly woman as a prank. The woman catches and subdues him (don't mess with an ex-Marine!). Instead of handing the boy over to the police, she decides to teach him some manners.

☐   A teen's little sister ruins what's supposed to be a perfect date in the most adorable, hilarious way possible. The date goes better than perfect as a result.

☐ Jim and Sonia are getting divorced. Their families are trying to be supportive, but it's proving difficult - mostly because neither Jim nor Sonia seem to need any supporting. The couple is perfectly happy. In fact, they say they're getting divorced because their marriage was getting in the way of their friendship.

Write a scene around the divorce, in whatever way you wish. Make sure to include lots of banter between the ex-couple, and confusion among the onlookers.

☐ Having a hedgehog for a pet is nothing uncommon. Having your grumpy, cynical roommate *turn into* a hedgehog is an adventure - mostly in retaining your sanity.

That, and witch-hunting.

☐ Rewrite a scene from a dramatic work in a humorous/satirical tone.

Examples of works you could use:

- Homer's *The Iliad*
- Dante's *Inferno*
- Shakespeare's *Hamlet*

☐ A mother overhears one of her children talking on the phone, and completely misinterprets the conversation.

☐ Write a sweet, funny tale of a young child taking care of their baby brother/sister.

☐ Write a story centered around working in an office, "Office" style (the TV show). Make all the workers supernatural creatures.

☐ Write a story featuring a seemingly senseless character getting into hilarious trouble with dangerous people. Have the character turn out to be the smartest man/woman in story at the very end.

☐ A fool for a King should make a kingdom easy pickings for an enemy or greedy nobility looking to overturn the crown, right? Wrong. The King of Sudnik is not simply foolish - he is the luckiest fool to ever have lived, and anyone who dares stand against him learns at their own peril what it means to be favored by the Fates. Dastardly plans are thwarted in hilarious and embarrassing ways, while the people of Sudnik cheer for their empty-headed, none-the-wiser ruler.

☐ Write a script for a scene in a comedy TV show. Premise: The teacher's lounge in a public high school.

☐ A villain crosses into an alternate universe, where the superheroes and super-villains of his world are fictional. He is ecstatic - taking over the world should be a piece of cake, with no one able to stand against him or match his power! Now, if the villain could only escape getting mobbed by fangirls thinking him the actor who'd played his character in a recent movie, he might actually get something done.

☐ A man picks a fight with someone way out of his league. The consequences are...less dire than he might have expected, given the kind of people he'd inadvertently angered.

Housekeeping for a mafia clan beats ending in a shallow grave, right?

☐ Years of bad karma culminate in one spectacularly awful day for a greedy businessman. What is supposed to be the realization of decades of behind-the-scenes machinations turns into something else instead. Cameras are rolling, and the whole world bears witness to the man's inglorious fall from grace.

Bonus points: Fit as many humor gags (pie in face, stepping on a rake, etc.) as you possibly can into this tale.

☐   A man keeps making a fool out of himself in front of the person he likes.

Write the story as a collection of scenes, with the last scene holding the resolution. Does the man finally gain his crush's attention?

☐   Loving your greatest rival isn't easy. Take a love-hate relationship to the max; make the characters in question impossible to reconcile - for example, a superhero and a super-villain. Take the perspective of the less likeable of the two. Have them struggle with their feelings, and think their crush one-sided - until the very end, when they discover their feelings are returned.

☐   A man is suddenly given the ability to enter other people's dreams when he himself is asleep. He sets out to play harmless pranks to those who annoy him during his waking hours.

☐   The CEO of a certain multi-billion company and his right-hand man are known to bicker constantly and viciously, regardless of whether they are in private or public. They are best friends and make one heck of a team.

☐ Depict a day in the life of a receptionist. Rude visitors, absentminded employees, and general strangeness of passerby abound.

☐ A scatter-minded woman often finds random animals in her home. Other people's cats, dogs, and - that one memorable time - snakes sneak in, usually led inside by the woman herself while she is busy doing something else.

☐ A man tries to hold it together during a meeting at work as his boss' toupee slides further and further down the man's head, ruffled by the breeze coming from an open window.

☐ A normally standoffish college student becomes affectionate and goofy when really tired. His roommates are endlessly amused at his expense every exam season.

☐ A family finds black-and-white photographs of a great-great-grandparent. The photos are not what they would have expected. They are all really silly and sweet, illuminating the character of a person most of them had never met.

☐ A spell is miscast, with hilarious results.

☐ A witch turns people who displease her into frogs. The frogs in question retain distinguishing characteristics of the people they had been, such as hairstyle and even the clothes the person had been wearing. They also speak, albeit half in croaks.

☐ Two teens are discussing someone in their native language, and are being none too charitable. Little do they know, the victim of their gossip is fluent in that language. She/he makes them aware of the fact in a most hilarious fashion.

☐ An arrogant man, self-appointed member of the "intelligentsia," gets stuck in a provincial town in the middle of nowhere. To say he rubs people the wrong way would be putting his ineptitude mildly. The locals take to making fun of him instead of getting angry, an approach that goes over the man's head in hilarious ways.

☐ Do a funny review of a terrible book, movie, or TV show you have seen recently. Style it as one of the characters making fun of their fictional world.

☐ A chef working at a high-end restaurant gets an ingredient wrong in a meal meant for an extremely important client. The result is unpalatable. The chef realizes his mistake, but the dish is already out on the floor. The chef quickly organizes the staff into sabotaging the meal before the client can take a bite.

☐ A man finds his great-grandfather's diary while cleaning his parents' house. The great-grandfather in question is remembered for being a very strict, tough man. The diary gives the man a different perspective of his relative. His great-grandfather had a lighter side, and a wicked sense of humor.

☐ A man and a woman meet at a charity gala. They arrange for a date the following evening, having liked the other's company - or rather, their apparent wealth. Both are in fact con artists who make their living by swindling romantic partners out of their money. Their date is comedic in its theatrics, with neither party being genuine with their affections.

☐ An aged married couple argues while purchasing tickets at the cinema. Write the story from the perspective of the young couple waiting in line behind them.

☐ The most popular kid in school falls for a girl who is all things he is not. In a bid to impress her, he joins the school's poetry club and attempts to craft a poem worthy of her notice. The results are....hilarious.

☐ Puff, the family cat, gets especially creative when seeking vengeance. None dare insult her twice.

☐ Rewrite a well-known folk tale as a comedy. Have the villain be the main character. Make them hilariously inept at whatever they are doing, but completely certain of their superiority. The hero should be only slightly more competent, and possibly even less intelligent.

☐ A young child sneaks into an animal enclosure at the zoo, befriends the inhabitants, and generally has the time of their life before the inevitable, panicky discovery.

☐   A family travels back to their native country/ city after many years away. The family's children were young when the family departed. Now in their teens, they do not remember their relatives very well. The time they spend with their grandparents and various aunts and uncles and cousins makes two things clear to them: First, genes are a scary thing - there are certain traits and quirks the teens can trace from their grandparents through their parents, to their own selves.

Second, they have the most awesome family ever.

☐   A man with a naturally grumpy disposition and a no-nonsense attitude is not-so-secretly despised at work. When the venue for the company's much-awaited New Year's party falls through, the man offers his home as an alternative. His coworkers are none too pleased, imagining a dry night of boring talk.

They could not have been more wrong.

☐   A group of tourists gets stranded in a remote village in a foreign country. The tourists do not speak the local language, and the village folk do not understand a word the tourists say. Both sides resort to charades to get their points across. Hilarious misunderstandings abound.

☐   Write a conversation between teenagers trying to appear "cool" from the point of view of an adult bystander. The observer is amused by the teens, and recalls his/her own teenage years with equal measures of fondness and embarrassment.

☐   Someone hacks into a high school's announcement system. The speakers now play poppy songs at random intervals.

☐   Jake is terrible at socializing. He speaks too frankly and directly for most people's tastes, resulting in frequent faux pas and embarrassing situations. When an invitation to a cousin's wedding comes in the mail, Jake resolves to use the occasion and widen his social circle.

Rather the opposite happens. Jake won't be getting invited to family gatherings for quite a time to come.

☐   Write a story in which all characters have strange, silly names. Don't address or explain this phenomenon. Make the story dialogue-heavy, mentioning names frequently.

☐ The star of a popular TV show decides to pursue a secondary passion - singing. Unfortunately, they can't sing worth a dime. The star's fans don't seem to mind, flocking to concerts and suffering through terrible acoustics without a murmur of protest.

In reality, the star is quite aware of their musical deficiency. Their attempt at a singing career had been calculated to lower their popularity and allow them to retire from show business. The unwavering support of their fanbase is both touching and incredibly frustrating.

☐ An office worker shares her lunch with a stray cat. When she returns home from work, she finds the stray at her doorsteps. The woman tries to ignore the uninvited visitor, but the feline is persistent and unfairly adorable. She eventually caves in and adopts the ball of fluff.

☐ Bad luck has dogged a man his entire life. When he wins an all-expenses paid trip to a luxurious hotel in a local lottery, the man thinks the streak of misfortune has finally broken. He is quickly proven wrong. Everything that can go wrong with the trip, does - and in a hilarious fashion. Dozens of small troubles pile up, making for the most exhausting vacation the man has ever taken.

☐   Kyle breaks his leg. He is given a month off from school to heal. His parents work during the day, there is nothing on TV, and internet is spotty in the mountainous area where he lives. Kyle is left to entertain himself by listening in on the local grandmothers, who gather to gossip at a bench right outside Kyle's house. He learns more about the town and its inhabitants than he ever wanted to know.

☐   Write a scene set in a supermarket, during the busiest time of the day. A parent is trying to get their grocery shopping done for the week, wrangle two mischievous children, and dodge overly-helpful staff.

☐   A man receives a call from his boss early in the morning. The man hasn't had his coffee yet, and ends up being way more frank in answering his boss' questions regarding a current project than is necessarily smart. The man spends the commute to work thinking he will be fired on sight.

He is promoted instead.

☐   Three monks enter a bar...

But really, three monks, in a bar. The regular patrons don't know what to make of their presence. The monks spin a curious tale - a story that is eventually proven false when the cops burst in, seeking what turn out to be three criminals in disguise.

☐   Two friends have a fight over something stupid, and vow to never be friends again. Both regret their words. Each organizes something outlandish in order to win the other's forgiveness.

 # ETECTIVE

Detective fiction offers a mystery and challenges the reader to solve it. Whether you are writing a cozy mystery or a hard-boiled crime novel, you will find a case worthy of your detective's attention in the prompts below.

☐ A private detective is hired to find the missing daughter of a wealthy CEO. The detective finds a whole bunch of other missing things (lost pets, stolen diamonds, a secret agent) during his/her investigation, but there's no sign of the CEO's brat.

The CEO's daughter isn't missing - she ran away from home in a fit of boredom. The girl is following the detective around in different disguises, and generally having the time of her life.

☐ What does a detective do, after catching the most notorious thief of their time?

Why, break the thief out of jail, of course.

☐ Sarah can't find her earrings. The suspect: short, hairy, and prone to filching shiny things. Sarah ransacks the house, and finds way more than her earrings in her cat's treasure stashes. Some of the loot doesn't even belong to her! Like, say, that huge rock that kind of looks like a ruby...

☐ The largest casino in Las Vegas is robbed, losing several million dollars in a single night. The detectives investigating the case believe it to be an inside job. They also suspect mob connections. The casino stays open, with agents working undercover.

☐ A jogger finds not one, not two, but *three* dead bodies during their morning runs over the course of a couple of months. The police is getting awfully suspicious. The jogger him/herself is innocent, and quite appalled at their terrible luck.

☐ A squirrel detective investigates the theft of a stash of nuts. Among those suspected: An old crow whose distinctive hacking was heard before the stash went missing; a fat house cat who lives to make trouble for everyone else; a sleepy hedgehog, passing through the squirrel's turf on his way to the forest.

☐   Sean's penchant for getting into trouble makes him a natural suspect when a security guard finds a bag of coke stuffed in the empty locker next to his. Sean isn't guilty. There is no proof and the school eventually drops the investigation, but everyone seems to think Sean was involved.

Sean lost a family member to drugs. He's in absolute rage over the case, and resolves to find the punk responsible on his own. Nobody's selling coke in *his* school.

☐   A cop working undercover in a gang disappears. His gang-mates who approach the police, looking for help in locating the man. While the police scrambles to organize a search party without further compromising the investigation, the cop's fiancée hires a private detective. She sets him after the cop's partner in the force.

☐   A man discovers he has an older brother. The man is in his thirties. Both of his parents are dead, and he isn't close to any of his remaining relatives. There is no one he can ask why such an enormous thing had been kept from him for so long - no one except his absent brother.

The man resolves to find his sibling - a tall order, seeing as the man turns out to be a criminal wanted for murder.

☐   Kara was a troubled teen. Petty theft, disorderly behavior, and other small crimes got her well-acquainted with her local police precinct. She even spent a year in juvie at sixteen.

That's all in the past now. Kara is working while studying for a Master's degree. Her old life seems like a distant dream - a dream that turns into a very real nightmare when one of Kara's old acquaintances shows up at her door. This friend has serious dirt on Kara, and uses it to blackmail Kara into helping him/her find a third friend who has gone missing. Kara must now play detective and keep the whole sordid case on the down-low from both the police and the people in her life.

☐   A member of the royal family has been kidnapped. By accident.

Write the tale of a bewildered duo of car thieves who find an unexpected passenger in the trunk. The royal in question is out cold - apparently, someone *else* had been in the middle of kidnapping them, when the car thieves snuck away with the getaway vehicle. Now the poor men have to figure out a way to get the royal back where they belong without getting caught - either by the police, or the *actual* kidnappers.

☐   A human trafficking case leads a detective to a powerful underground crime group. The detective is able to join the group, and is doing his best to track down the victim from within. He gains the group's trust and slowly begins to move up the ranks. As he does, he sees his fair share of illegal dealings - and recognizes not a few of the dirty cops in the group's clutches. The detective is making good progress.

Until a familiar face threatens to blow his cover to hell.

☐   A worthless painting is stolen from the home of an ordinary, blue-collar family. The police can't do much, as good as dismissing the case. The family is more spooked by the intrusion into their home than having something so frivolous stolen. However, there is more to the crime than meets the eye. Enough, in fact, to capture the attention of the brilliant detective living across the street from the burglarized family.

☐   Shannon has a secret admirer. Gifts and letters make their anonymous way to her desk week after week. She is slowly putting the clues of who the sender might be together.

☐ A car skids off the road in a remote, snowy town deep in the mountains. The car is totaled. The driver seeks help, and is set up in a local house to wait out a winter storm that is tying up the roads and her rescue. It will be at least a week until safe travel is possible.

The stranded woman fears boredom initially. She soon finds the town much more exciting than is necessarily healthy. Strange things happen around her, but no one seems to be paying them any mind. The woman loves detective novels and starts running her own investigation into the proceedings. Is there anything to her worries, or is she jumping at shadows?

☐ A child disappears, leaving no trace behind. Her family is devastated. They never stop looking for the girl, even when everyone else does.

A year later, the missing girl's elder sibling finds a child's shoe near a place the girl used to frequent. They are convinced it belongs to their lost sister.

The tiny clue breaks the whole case open.

☐ A dorm room suffers the attention of a food thief. But not for long! A sleep-deprived Criminology student is on the case. Nobody steals *her* coffee without some serious consequences.

☐ An aged detective takes on an apprentice. The detective is famous the world over; many had vied for a spot as his pupil over the years, with no success. The young woman he chooses to teach is nothing anyone would have expected. Egos are hurt all around, among them those of some very important people.

☐ Dead bodies start disappearing from morgues across the city. Have the reason be as unexpected and twisted as possible. Feel free to introduce cross-genres, such as fantasy or horror.

☐ A woman has her identity stolen online. Only the criminals have the wrong person this time; the woman in question is a black-hat hacker, and they've painted themselves as targets.

☐ A series of petty crimes occur at a prime resort in Florida. The local police and resort security take their time with the cases. Meanwhile, an off-duty detective on vacation with his family in that same resort begins his own investigation. The detective is convinced the minor crimes are serving as decoys, and that something much larger is on its way.

☐ A man has his mail stolen. He doesn't notice at first, but when a month goes without a single letter or flyer making it to his mailbox, he finally catches on. But who could be taking the mail? And why?

☐ A man obsessed with the disappearance of a close childhood friend continues to pursue the case as a grown man, now a detective on the police force. Every once in a while, he would find a clue. One such puzzle piece appears in a murder case that lands on the man's desk.

☐ Write a who-dun-it style detective story, with the twist of the culprit being the detective him/herself.

☐ A retired detective receives letters from an unknown sender. The letters come once a week. Each contains a photo, and a name typed onto an otherwise blank sheet of paper. The detective thinks the letters may be threats, but directed at whom? And why? The people in the pictures are not related to each other in any way that he can discern.

☐ A lock of hair in a golden locket is the sole clue a detective has in a case involving the murder of a high-ranking politician.

☐   A criminal escapes prison. Write a story from the criminal's perspective as they attempt to avoid the law. Focus on their motivation and the precautions they take not to be detected.

☐   Naomi believes a classmate has stolen her diary, which contains a number of embarrassing secrets. She breaks into that classmate's locker, and finds something that makes her forget about her missing diary.

☐   A family member never makes it to Thanksgiving dinner, despite having confirmed attendance and called before starting their journey. A frantic search reveals their car abandoned by the side of the road, not far from the family's house. There is no trace of the driver, or clues as to their whereabouts.

☐   A notorious criminal falls in love with the detective who has been dogging his heels. The criminal begins to leave little presents for the detective on each crime scene, teasing his crush and the authorities with clues about his true identity.

☐ A little girl "hires" the detective who lives next door to find her missing doll. The detective takes the job. The search for the missing Barbie leads him somewhere unexpected.

☐ A child disappears from its family home. The house has been broken into, with the parents unaware until the following morning, when they discover their son/daughter is missing.

Something does not add up about the situation. The detective assigned to the case concludes that the break-in has been staged, and suspects the parents involved. The motive and the child's fate are unclear.

☐ Bodies missing their ring fingers keep popping up across a large metropolitan town. A detective on the case is trying to figure out the killer's motive and identity.

☐ A hardened detective has been forcibly retired after a particularly difficult case left him with a bullet in the shoulder. He is not exactly enjoying a peaceful retirement, opting to instead solve every mystery or crime to come to his attention, no matter how small. His neighbors are getting a little peeved, all things told.

☐ A music box goes missing from the home of an elderly woman. The box contains several important keepsakes, and the woman is anxious to see it returned. She hires a detective to track down the thief.

The detective finds their work cut out for them. The music box and its contents appear worthless, other than their sentimental value - something a thief wouldn't appreciate.

Or would they? Who is the thief, and what is their motivation?

☐ A multi-million dollar company goes bankrupt, seemingly overnight. The CEO and his cabinet are ruined; several men take their own lives. The cause of the company's sudden downfall is more sinister than the merciless workings of the markets. The official investigation is incomplete, and most seem more interested in covering up the whole case and associated scandals than finding out the truth.

A former employee takes matters into their own hands and launches an investigation of their own.

☐ An eighty-year-old woman stuns the world by solving the crime mystery of the century. How did she do it? Who was the culprit?

☐ A million-dollar necklace goes missing. So does the woman who was wearing it. Her husband appears more concerned about the jewelry. The detective in charge of the case is struggling to maintain professional objectivity in face of his/her extreme dislike of the negligent husband.

☐ The robbery of a jewelry store leaves the police baffled. The state-of-the-art security system wasn't tipped during the heist, nor did any of the numerous cameras catch a glimpse of trouble. The jewelry simply appears to disappear between one hour and the next.

☐ A teen who is often bullied at school stops coming to class. The classmates who used to bully him seem to care the most about his absence, their worry motivated in no small amount by guilt over their behavior. Since no one seems to be doing anything to find the boy, the group decides to take the matter into their own hands.

☐ Fire burns through a forest. A nearby town will profit from the disaster, as the burned land can now be used for farming. The police suspects foul play and sends a detective to investigate.

☐   An incredibly expensive diamond ring disappears during a dinner party. The ring is a family heirloom, showcased in a prime location within the host's mansion. The host discovers it missing halfway through the party, and immediately alerts the authorities. The house is put on lockdown and the guests forbidden from leaving until the ring is found.

Twist: None of the guests stole the ring. Come up with an unusual cause for its disappearance.

☐   A rundown mill in a small town is believed to be haunted. The place is near collapsing, but resides on private land and the owner refuses to have it torn down. Parents forbid their children from going near the building. Many still sneak inside, hoping to catch a glimpse of something supernatural.

One such group of kids becomes a witness to something else instead. Someone has recently moved into the mill - a stranger to the town, whose purpose there is unknown.

☐   Notes are being left around the city, each warning of a particular crime a day before it is committed. A detective attempts to figure out the identity of the sender and his/her connection to the crimes.

☐ Write a story about a crime-solving cat and its pet, a human detective.

☐ A detective investigating a case discovers the criminal's identity, but empathizes too deeply with their motives to bring them to justice.

☐ A man is found gruesomely murdered. The victim had been acquitted from a heinous crime thirty years prior - a detail of some relevance, as the man was killed on the anniversary of his acquittal. The police naturally suspects the accuser in that old case. He/she has a solid alibi, but appears much too happy with the news of the man's death.

☐ The lights in a house flicker every night at the same hour. A neighbor is convinced that someone inside the house is using Morse code in an attempt to communicate with the outside world without detection. The neighbor begins to make notes of the perceived signals, and discovers their suspicions are correct.

☐ When a community is swindled by con-artists playing at contractors, they bond together to find the criminals and bring them to justice.

☐ Projects made by a particular student keep disappearing from their classroom. The teacher, suspecting bullying, begins to keep a close eye on her class. She discovers the culprit, but their motivations are not what the teacher had expected.

☐ Teenagers are running away from home at an unprecedented rate. Police in the affected area are baffled; many of the missing teens have no apparent cause for discontent, either at home or at school. An investigation eventually discovers the teens. They are all together, and involved in something unexpected.

☐ A notorious thief is caught after over a decade of successfully evading law enforcement. The detective who had been leading the investigation is highly suspicious over the easy capture. His doubts are eventually proven correct, as the thief pulls off his greatest heist yet - all thanks to law enforcement's unwilling aid.

AIRY TALES

Children around the world grow up with fairy tales and myths of fantastical creatures, powerful deities, and miracles of all kinds. Capture the wonder and wisdom of this genre with the prompts below!

☐   A girl finds out she has rather....extraordinary parentage. Of the lightning-wielding, Viking kind. That is *after* she comes into her magical inheritance and nearly burns down her high school.

☐   Sleeping Beauty wakes up not to her love's kiss, but the sound of bulldozers. She has slept a *lot* longer than the evil witch had wagered.

    The witch is dead, the spell is broken, and a princess from a time of fairies and kings wakes up in modern-day Europe.

☐   Write a Human tale - a story that fairy-tale creatures tell their young ones, to warn them about the evils of humans.

☐   Vampire lore tells of an unusual way to combat a blood-sucker: Spilling a bag of seeds, pebbles, or anything scatter-prone in a vampire's presence is said to stop the creature in its tracks. The tasty human a vampire is pursuing is momentarily forgotten in favor of counting the loose grains.

Include this somewhat silly aspect of vampirism in a tale of an elegant, Victorian-era vampire.

☐   A deity on the run from an evil force hides their soul in a mortal child. Twenty years later, the deity's soul awakens in their now adult host. It is time to pick up the chase again, this time as the one hunting the evil. The human body is a bit of a deterrent, but not enough to stop an immortal once their mind is made up.

The human soul sharing said body is taken along for the ride.

☐   There are no mermaids. MerMEN do exist, however. They tend to be very obnoxious, what with all the pulling sailors into the sea for laughs and whistling at people walking along the shore.

☐ In Greek mythology, King Minos had a labyrinth built to contain the Minotaur - a powerful man with the head of a bull. The Minotaur is depicted as a vicious monster. The hero Theseus eventually slays the Minotaur, but not before the creature kills and consumes a great number of innocent women and men, offered in tribute by King Minos himself.

Write a tale along the premises of King Minos' Labyrinth and the Minotaur. Set it in the modern day, devoid of fantastical elements.

☐ The Association of Fairy Tale Villains has its first meeting. Who attends? What are the panels and topics of discussion? Who is picketing in front of the auditorium?

☐ Take a well-known fairy tale, and flip the genders of all characters involved. How would the tale change?

Stories you could use:

- Little Red Riding Hood
- Ali Baba and the Forty Thieves
- The Little Mermaid

☐   Ragnarök is a time of both destruction and rebirth in Norse mythology. Great gods will fall. War and natural disasters will ravage the earth, until finally all is swallowed by water.

Ragnarök is not the end of all things. The event signifies a break in the old cycle and the beginning of a new one - a clean slate. The world will emerge from the sea more beautiful and fertile. A new kind of people will repopulate Earth, while new gods rise to power. Write a tale set in the aftermath of Ragnarök, either from the point of view of a surviving god or a human walking the new earth.

☐   Set a tale in a land where supernatural creatures are the normal residents, and humans - the things of fairy tales.

☐   The gods have come down to Earth. That is, all gods to have ever existed in human stories. They are fascinated by how human culture has evolved and - after outlawing war and ensuring everyone's living standard goes up just by being a huge, magical deterrent to evil - decide to spend some time among us.

Cue strange game shows such as, "Date a god for a day." Your character is the lucky winner of one such blind date, with a deity of your choosing.

☐ Choose a fairy tale. Rewrite it as to exclude magic, with each fantastical character transformed into an appropriate real-world equivalent. You may select whatever time period you like as the setting of your story.

Note: Charlotte Bronte's Jane Eyre *would be an example, which references "Beauty and the Beast."*

☐ A high school puts on a play written by students. In the script, a character fake-summons an ancient god.

The summoning turns out to be legitimate, but incomplete. The god appears without a body or anyone's notice. He/she slips into one of the students. The student in question *does* notice, but is afraid to tell anyone. Meanwhile, the reborn deity proves a little more mischievous and crime-orientated than their mortal host is willing to tolerate.

☐ Cats truly have nine lives. They remember them, too.

The hero of your story is a cat. It spends each of its nine lives protecting its very first owner, then his children after the man's death.

☐ A girl falls through a crack in the human realm, and ends up somewhere else entirely. The sky is black, the earth is black, the forest she is wandering through glistens in shades of onyx and obsidian... Not to mention the strange creatures skittering in the underbrush. The place screams, "hell" - quite literally.

Having more or less accepted her fate, the girl starts wondering about the pragmatics - what she will do about food, where she might find shelter, that sort of thing. She is also growing more and more curious as to which version of the underworld she is exploring.

☐ A witch steals a young child and makes him her apprentice, as per witchy tradition. The witch binds the child to her magic before realizing it is male. She "fixes" her mistake by raising the boy as a girl, far away from other humans and with no reference for the boy to think anything strange.

Fast forward ten years. A passing knight stumbles onto the witch's hut and, believing the young girl inside to be a prisoner, takes the witch's apprentice away - quite against the boy's will. The apprentice hasn't gotten the hang of magic just yet. Being male may have something to do with why his spells keep misfiring. The knight thinks the young man a maiden. Things spin off the road from there.

☐ Mari wants to meet a dragon. Never mind that dragons breathe fire and eat people and are, by all accounts, fictional. She has made up her mind, and won't give up until she finds a dragon of her own to cuddle.

Meanwhile, a local hen is trying to figure out where the giant egg in her nest came from and how exactly to go about warming it so it will hatch.

☐ The tomb of an ancient warrior has been disturbed. The warrior's ghost manifests, and sets to haunt the person responsible for disturbing the warrior's rest.

The person in question is possibly the most lovable human being to have ever existed. Ghost or not, the warrior is too charmed to do any proper haunting. He ends up tailing the young human and helping them out whenever they found themselves in a tricky situation.

☐ Legend says that eating the flesh of a mermaid grants one immortality.

A young noble is tricked into consuming mermaid flesh. He/she lives to see the world they had known die, to be rebuilt into something else.

☐   A young girl is lost in an urban city. Her parents are beyond themselves with worry. They have the police looking out for her, terrified something has happened. The girl makes it home by midnight the same day she had gone missing. She is unharmed, and insists that a fox had shown her the way back home.

☐   Choose a fairy tale creature. Give them a flaw that would make them terrible at doing what is expected of their kind.

Examples:

- A witch who is allergic to magic.
- A fairy afraid of flying/heights
- A siren who can't sing.

☐   A man sneaks up on a beautiful woman while she bathes in a lake. Her clothes are on the shore; he steals them, believing the woman a Selkie - a creature who turns human when she sheds her skin, and can be possessed by the one who holds the skin itself. The woman is not a Selkie. Neither is she a woman.

The river god is not happy about the thieving human on his territory.

☐ A man grabs the wrong pair of boots on his way out of a village pub. It's dark out, the night dreary with rain, and the man doesn't realize his mistake until he is on his horse and half-way to a neighboring town. The boots are scruffy and a bit worn over the toes. The man figures he hasn't really done the owner such a grave injustice; the pair he'd left behind were in a much better condition.

Except the boots are not ordinary - there is a spell on them, making the wearer swift on foot and luck. The boots' owner is not a nice man. He very much wants them back, by any means necessary.

☐ A contemporary human meets a mythological creature, and finds them much different from what folktales say.

☐ Hansel and Gretel don't stumble onto a house made of candy. Instead, they find their way to the doorstep of a good witch. The witch is not pleased to learn how the two children had come to be lost in her forest.

☐   "The Boy who Drew Cats" is a strange, amusing tale of a boy who couldn't stop drawing cats. The boy's obsession with felines eventually saves both his life and the livelihood of his village.

Write a short story that features a hero who, by pursuing his/her passion, is able to defeat some great evil. Make the story suitable for young readers, and as fun and unexpected as possible.

☐   An ancient prophecy is misinterpreted, and the wrong man is put on the throne. The error is discovered - to the chagrin of the real heir and savior of the kingdom, who had been rather enjoying life without the crushing weight of responsibility on his shoulders. Or fairy tale creatures seeking help at every turn.

☐   Pick two characters from different mythological works. Have them meet and interact, with the main action of the tale driven by either attraction or conflict between them.

☐   What became of Little Red Riding Hood, after the whole fiasco with the Big Bad Wolf and her granny? Write a sequel to the story, with Little Red now a not-so-well-adjusted young adult.

☐   Vampires have a long history in mythology. Before Dracula was ever penned, vampire-like creatures stalked heroes in Greek and Roman myths and terrorized villages in Asia.

Research a type of ancient vampire. Insert the creature in a modern setting, and tell a story of a human encounter with its kind.

☐   A siren responsible for many a shipwreck is captured by sailors. The sailors cut out the siren's tongue and haul her ashore, to become a pet amusement for the kingdom's monarch.

The siren may be mute, but she is not without a trick up her scaly sleeves. She regains her tongue - or rather, *a* tongue - and finds true power in dominion over the kingdom's ruler.

☐   The Loch Ness monster is real. Nessy loves humans - so much so that she lives among them, with no one ever the wiser. Water reveals her true form, so she tries to stay away from wet places when out and about in the human world.

☐ A faceless ghost haunts a hotel that has been the site of several deaths in the past year. The ghost is not the killer, but one of the victims. The medium/detective trying to solve the case must figure out who the ghost is first - to see their face, so to speak - in order to solve the mystery of the killings.

Mythological creature responsible for the deaths: noppera-bo (Japanese yōkai)

☐ Foxes can change their appearance, at times assuming human guise in order to trick unwitting mortals. A man able to see through their illusions turns the tables and plays a trick on a mischievous fox.

☐ The Moon Goddess, Kuu, drops a precious ring down on Earth. The ring grants its owner infinite wisdom.

What would the ring be worth, in the hands of an illiterate peasant?

☐ A supernatural creature falls in love with a human after listening to them sing.

☐ Telling ghost stories with friends is a pleasant way to spend hot summer nights. It is important that the number of stories told in a single night never reaches 100, however; legend holds that the hundredth tale will call to something beyond the human realm, and bring misfortune to those gathered.

☐ Kappa are creatures in Japanese mythology. They live in lakes and rivers, and are known to drown or gut unexpected humans. Their one weakness? They must be wet at all times, or they lose their strength. To that end, Kappa carry water in a bowl-like depression atop their heads. Get a Kappa to bow and spill the water, and you might just escape their wrath.

Write a story featuring a Kappa and a traveler who happens upon the Kappa's home.

☐ Margaret's neighbor is a giant. Margaret is a witch herself, although she doesn't go around advertising the fact. Her neighbor somehow learns of her magical disposition; he wishes to be human-sized, and won't stop bothering her for a magical "cure" to his giant-ness.

☐   Human worship of Halloween has led to the birth of a new deity. This new godling has no lore, no name, and no specific powers. The deity makes their first appearance one Hallow's Eve, in the midst of a big Halloween party held in New York City.

☐   Choose a fairy tale you know by heart. Switch the perspective to a side character, and retell the story.

For example...

• How did the magical tale of Cinderella go, according to one of her step-sisters?

• What did Gerda's mother do when her daughter disappeared in search of the missing Kai? (Tale: Hans Christian Andersen's *The Snow Queen*)

• What motivated the bandit leader in *Ali Baba and the Forty Thieves*? What happened to him and his men after the tale of Ali Baba ended - that is, once they were in the Sultan's custody?

☐   An evil queen struggles to hold onto her ill-gotten kingdom. Write the tale from the queen's perspective as she battles heroes and intrigues in her own Court.

☐ The ugly duckling doesn't grow to be a swan, but a phoenix. As few such creatures remain in the mortal world, the young phoenix remains unaware of its true nature even as an adult. That is, until an encounter with a human dogged by misfortune calls upon the magic that burns within the otherworldly bird.

☐ There are tales of floating kingdoms - strange lands seen only in glimpses, drifting far in the heavens or shrouded in mist on dark seas.

Misfortune sends a character stumbling into one such place. The character is alone, with no easy way to return home. He/she finds peace in life removed from all worries and troubles. However, the character cannot forget one particular person he/she has left behind.

☐ Choose a mythological creature that is ghastly in form, but benevolent in nature. Write a tale about a human's encounter with that particular creature.

Mythological creatures to consider, and their land of origin:

- The Scorpion Man, Babylon
- Tengu, Japan
- Ichthyocentaurs, Greece

☐ An actress playing a princess in a movie adaptation of a fairy tale wakes up in the world of the story she is portraying on the big screen.

☐ Japanese legends hold that when an object reaches an age of 100 years, it becomes animated. Write a tale of an everyday object that gains awareness on its 100th birthday. Set the tale in modern times, and choose an object that would realistically be at hand for your protagonist.

☐ A skin-walker makes her home near a small town. She plays dangerous tricks on the town's inhabitants, and hides her presence by transfiguring into various animals. Her games lead to death and destruction.

The only person who is aware of what is happening is reluctant to expose the witch. There are secrets buried in the town; its residents are far from innocent, and those who are hurt by the skin-walker may well deserve their fate.

☐ A young girl is swept away from shore while on an outing with her friends. She loses consciousness; when she wakes up again, she is in an underwater city built and populated by a mythological race of people some call the Yacuruna.

☐　　Choose two folk or fairy tales that originate from two different cultures. Write a story that incorporates both myths, and their main characters.

Possible combinations:

- *The Sleeping Prince* (Greece) and *Aladdin* (Persia)

- *Rumpelstiltskin* (Germany) and *Momotaro* (Japan)

- *Bluebeard* (France) and *Snegurochka* (Russia)

 ANTASY

Fantastical stories capture the imagination and delight the reader in unexpected ways. The prompts below will whisk you to wondrous lands, or challenge you to find the extraordinary in the everyday.

☐   A tiny snow fairy is accidentally swept into a woman's hair, and whisked into a human dwelling. The fairy breaks one of its wings in the process. The woman discovers her unexpected guest and attempts to make the fairy comfortable while the poor creature's wing heals.

☐   A terrible accident greatly damages Jeanine's sight. Or so the doctors say. Jeanine can't see the world anymore - not as she had known it before the accident. People appear to her as shadows.

The humanoid creatures moving around and through them, on the other hand, are perfectly clear.

☐ Every witch has a Familiar - a fantastical creature that offers companionship and protection. Familiars appear early on in a witch's life, usually in childhood. It is rare for a witch to reach adulthood without meeting his or her Familiar.

It's rarer still for a witch to turn twenty and not know they are a witch at all...

☐ Guardian spirits protect humans. Not all humans have a Guardian, and no human is aware of the Guardians' existence.

One Guardian finds an exception to the rule in the tiny, temperamental brat he is assigned to protect.

☐ Eileen is the only human in a city populated by otherworldly creatures. Not that she knows it - her parents are yet to tell her she's adopted. And here she thought she was just weird-looking...

Recommended genre: humor.

☐ Choose a fantastical creature, or create one yourself. Have this creature try to befriend a human in an outlandish way.

☐   A boy grows up with a reflection that doesn't match what other people see when they look at him. He thinks something must be wrong with him, and keeps his mismatched reflection a secret.

Until he meets a girl whose mirror shows a monster, too.

☐   A man was born with a strange affliction: He always says the opposite of what he means. Misunderstandings and misfortune dog the man his whole life. At thirty, he's finally had enough. The man decides to seek a cure, chasing stories of supernatural beings and deities throughout the land.

Write a story of one encounter the man has with a supernatural creature/deity. Don't forget - the man can only speak in "opposites."

☐   When Julie posted an ad for a roommate in the local paper, she didn't expect a goddess to come knocking on her door.

No, seriously. An actual goddess. (Lore of your choosing)

☐   Sherry's mother is a dragon. Accordingly, Sherry has a very different view of the world than most first-graders.

☐   A grumpy wizard finds a young child wandering through his forest. In the middle of a thunderstorm. Being chased by wolves.

The wizard takes the child to his home, planning to send him off on his way once the storm passes. Little does he know, a very dangerous man is looking for the boy, meaning to end the royal line with the child.

The wizard's life is about to get a lot more interesting.

☐   A small bakery offers their customers more than sugary, flaky goodness - they make dreams into tasty treats! Patrons are served their own dearest wishes, in the sweetest possible form. Eating one of the bakery's creations suffuses one with the courage and drive they need to make their wants a reality.

Even when doing so is a very, very stupid idea.

☐   Lena is the first human child to be born in over two hundred years. Her supernatural family has no idea what to do. The entire town - composed of witches, werewolves, vampires, and all kinds of creepy-crawly things - grows protective of their tiny, soft, human charge.

☐   A girl who can see the future tries her best to prevent the bad things she foresees from happening. Her sight is limited to a few days in advance, leaving her scrambling to reach people in need.

When someone close to her is in danger, she finds that her power is not limited to clairvoyance - and that its source is darker and its price, steeper than she could have ever imagined.

☐   In a world where magic and all things supernatural exist, a small subset of the human population is born with the ability to call upon and control dark creatures.

☐   The King of Hell is recruiting! Write an ad for a part-time job in the Underworld.

☐   A Fairy steals a child, leaving a Changeling in its place. The child's family raises the Fae child as their own, never suspecting anything amiss.

Ten years later, the Changeling gains its true nature. That same day, the stolen human child returns home, having broken free from the land of the Fae.

☐ A mermaid befriends a little girl. The two play together almost every day, for several years - until the girl suddenly stops coming to the sea. The mermaid waits and waits and waits.

When she can wait no more, she does something terrible to gain a human body and searches for her missing human friend.

☐ Write a humorous tale about time-traveling hi-jinks. There's no butterfly-effect to worry about - your characters are free to time-jump and mess with timelines without worrying they are changing their own time. Whatever the travelers do is undone as soon as they leave the specific period. The only catch: A time jump lasts only 15 minutes.

☐ Wishes do come true - if you are willing to pay their price. Set a story in a society where witches hold shop openly. Some are more powerful than others, and can perform real miracles. The rewards they demand are steep indeed.

☐ A strange creature whisks you to a world of fantastical beasts and magic. Write the story in first person point of view, present tense.

☐ In a world where every person is born with a grand purpose for being alive, a girl meant to rule the country meets another destined to bring the royal court to its knees. The royal Seer plays a dangerous game by telling neither of their fate.

☐ There is a window in grandmother's house that no one is allowed to open. Anita sits by it often, when she is bored of playing with her toys and the adults are not paying attention. The view outside changes every day, from snowy fields to a dry desert to forests lush with green.

☐ A monk saves a demon's life. The demon decides the monk is his to protect, ignoring the monk's heartfelt assurances that he would be perfectly fine without the evil presence dogging his every step.

☐ Create a spell, including the ritual and words that need to be spoken to make it work. What does your spell do? Who would use it?

☐ Elisa stumbles into a forgotten, dilapidated library where a tiny dragon has made a nest out of books and newspapers.

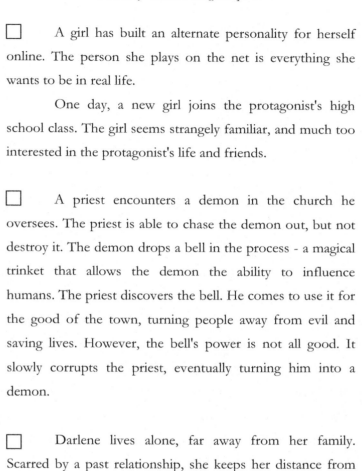

A girl has built an alternate personality for herself online. The person she plays on the net is everything she wants to be in real life.

One day, a new girl joins the protagonist's high school class. The girl seems strangely familiar, and much too interested in the protagonist's life and friends.

A priest encounters a demon in the church he oversees. The priest is able to chase the demon out, but not destroy it. The demon drops a bell in the process - a magical trinket that allows the demon the ability to influence humans. The priest discovers the bell. He comes to use it for the good of the town, turning people away from evil and saving lives. However, the bell's power is not all good. It slowly corrupts the priest, eventually turning him into a demon.

Darlene lives alone, far away from her family. Scarred by a past relationship, she keeps her distance from people in order to avoid getting hurt.

One day, Darlene receives a letter from someone she doesn't know. The letter is blank when she opens it. Thinking it a prank, Darlene discards the missive. The following morning, the letter is on her coffee table. As Darlene watches, words bleed into the page in black ink.

☐   The world of the Fae and the human world come into contact every fifty years, for one full day. During this time, Fae cross into the human world and get up to all kinds of mischief. They must be careful to mind the time, however, or they might be left behind when the portal closes.

The Fae Prince is not wont to limit the time he spends pursuing entertainment. His entourage loses sight of their princeling in the crucial moments before the portal closes.

☐   Tiny magical creatures infiltrate the modern human world. Not all can see them. Those who can find their living spaces infested and their daily lives much sillier. The creatures are not malicious, but they do have a flair for the dramatic and a very thin grasp on how human society works. Their magic mostly causes minor inconveniences - or, as the case may be, hugely embarrassing scenes for their human hosts.

☐   Shapeshifters have lived among humans for centuries. Most choose to remain in their animal forms while in the human world, keeping an eye on happenings in human society and at times influencing events in their favor.

☐ Simon is diagnosed with auditory dyslexia - a difficulty understanding spoken language. The disorder itself appears overnight; Simon is in his late thirties, and does not have a history of issues with language. He is not entirely convinced he does now, either. The auditory troubles he is having are not garbling up people's speech, but rather have Simon hearing words and sentences that do not belong in the flow of the conversation. Simon begins to suspect that what he is hearing are in fact pieces of people's thoughts.

☐ An ancient evil has been reborn. It seeks the key to the ten kingdoms - ten realms connected through the human world. The key itself was broken into pieces when the evil was defeated. Each piece is guarded by the descendants of those who initially fought the evil. As the story itself has long been lost, those in possession of the key's fragments are unaware that they are playing guardians to something incredibly important.

☐ Mia's mother is sick. Modern science has no answer, so Mia turns to the occult for help. She finds a cure for her mother - and is crowned queen of all the known worlds in the process.

☐ A witch opens a tattoo shop. She has all kinds of clients, both supernatural and human. One day, she mistakenly inks a magical tattoo onto a human. The tattoo moves and talks and is generally wont to blow the secret of the entire magical world.

The human in question had gotten the tattoo on a bet, while drunk; he wakes up to quite the surprise.

☐ Your character is the last of a line of Magic Bearers - people who act as mediums between the supernatural and human worlds. There can only be one Magic Bearer at a time; when the current holder of the title dies, your character is saddled with the responsibility of the position. As their mother had cut ties with her family long before your character was born, he/she is unaware of the sudden change in their life. Visits by strange creatures looking for help freak your character out almost as much as his/her newfound ability *to* help these otherworldly beings.

☐ What would a high-end restaurant ran by fantastical creatures look like? The restaurant is set in a human town, and visited by humans and strange(r) creatures alike. Are there separate menus? Are humans aware of the identity of the owners?

☐   A deity who eats dreams befriends a human. The deity decides to take a human form and come to know the human properly, in the waking world. Only the deity's friend doesn't appear to remember their friendship, or have any interest in the now-human deity.

☐   A farmer buys a magic potion to use on his plants. He is hoping to win first place at that year's garden festival with his homegrown pumpkins. Unfortunately for the farmer, the witch who sold him the potion has a very particular sense of humor. The result? Talking pumpkins. Sarcastic, talking pumpkins.

☐   Sammy is an only child. She lives in a big house with her parents, and is often lonely. One day, she decides to make up a friend for herself. The friend in question would live in Sammy's wardrobe, listen to all of her stories, and play with her when there is no one around.

Sammy's friend slowly becomes real. One day, a girl of Sammy's age crawls out of the wardrobe.

☐ Kira knows her sister is different. Her parents don't see it, their teachers don't see it, but Kira does - Clara is not fully human. As the two girls grow, Clara's real nature begins to show through. Kira is dedicated to protecting her sister from discovery at all costs.

☐ A deity is cursed into taking the form of a human. The deity in question abhors all of humanity, believing humans to be cruel and stupid creatures. Life among them teaches the deity that humans are a hundred other things besides - and that the good outweigh the bad.

☐ October is a spooky month. Spirits roam close to the earthly realm, waiting for the day the two briefly become one - Hallow's Eve. Humans carve pumpkins and stock up on candy. Spirits are similarly enthusiastic in their preparations for the occasion.

☐ A woman suffers a minor head injury. The next day, she wakes up to discover that everything in her house is animate - from the couch to the drapes and dishes. The coffee maker talks to her, the TV has an opinion on what is showing on the screen, and her darn mobile won't stop gossiping about her friends.

☐ While browsing the internet, Derek comes upon an ad for something called, "CharacterMorph." He clicks on the link out of curiosity, and is taken to a plain website featuring what appears to be a personality quiz. Derek finds himself answering questions on who he wants to be, rather than who he currently is. The quiz ends by asking Derek if he is sure he wants to enforce the selected changes. Derek thinks the whole thing a joke, and clicks "Yes."

☐ A troll moves into a small town. In true troll fashion, the creature makes its home under a bridge. Shortly thereafter, children begin to disappear. Supernatural creatures living in the area are quick to pin the series of crimes on the troll. The catch? The kidnappings aren't the troll's doing. In fact, the poor thing wants nothing to do with humans or their smelly kids. With elves and witches breathing down his neck, the troll has no choice but to find the real culprit.

☐ Maria buys a quaint mantle clock. It strikes every quarter hour, and counts off every full hour with a voice that echoes like a gong.

Unknown to Maria, a spell lies over the clock. Its voice is heard much farther than Maria's home, serving as a beacon for all kinds of strange creatures.

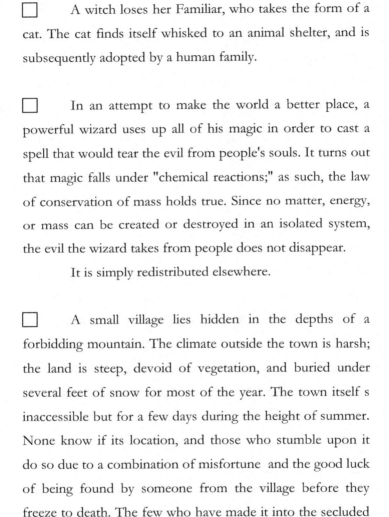

A witch loses her Familiar, who takes the form of a cat. The cat finds itself whisked to an animal shelter, and is subsequently adopted by a human family.

In an attempt to make the world a better place, a powerful wizard uses up all of his magic in order to cast a spell that would tear the evil from people's souls. It turns out that magic falls under "chemical reactions;" as such, the law of conservation of mass holds true. Since no matter, energy, or mass can be created or destroyed in an isolated system, the evil the wizard takes from people does not disappear.

It is simply redistributed elsewhere.

A small village lies hidden in the depths of a forbidding mountain. The climate outside the town is harsh; the land is steep, devoid of vegetation, and buried under several feet of snow for most of the year. The town itself s inaccessible but for a few days during the height of summer. None know if its location, and those who stumble upon it do so due to a combination of misfortune and the good luck of being found by someone from the village before they freeze to death. The few who have made it into the secluded settlement never return to their homes. They can't; those who see the village and the creatures that live within it are not permitted to leave.

ISTORICAL FICTION

History inspires all genres of writing. Knowledge of world history is invaluable in constructing rich stories and believable characters. The prompts in this section vary from fiction to nonfiction, and challenge the writer to expand the audience's understanding of the world.

☐ Choose two renowned philosophers. Write a conversation between them on a topic of interest.

Examples:

- Laozi and Thucydides, on the nature of war.
- Karl Marx and Ayn Rand, on social hierarchy.

☐ Write a tale of an early European expedition into the uncharted lands of present-day Canada.

☐ The South wins the American Civil War. Write a story set in present day, concerning the relationship between the two nations that form at the end of the war.

☐   Set a story during the forming days of a contemporary nation-state. You can focus the tale around a tribe's leader, perhaps the one responsible for the country's eventual creation, or an ordinary person settling a land with their family.

Countries of potential interest:

- Kingdom of Poland, est. 1025

- Nubia, est. ~ 2000BC

- China, Xia Dynasty (historical/fictional first dynasty), est. 2070BC

☐   Set a story in the Americas, before the Europeans arrived. Center it around a single native tribe. Keep to existing historical accounts of that tribe's customs and culture.

☐   Write a single scene from the life of a young family living during WWII. They are civilians and not a persecuted minority. The country they call home is one of the small European nations on the war's periphery. Nonetheless, the threat of destruction hangs heavy over the family's daily life.

☐   Write a sea tale inspired by a real-life female pirate, such as Ching Shih or Jeanne de Clisson. Have them run an all-female pirate ship, taunting the gods and men alike.

☐   Write a sweet romantic scene set in a historical era of your choosing.

☐   Write from the perspective of a servant in the employ of a historical figure.

Potential characters:

- A man in Caesar's household
- A maid serving Empress Cixi of China
- An attendant to Djosar, Egyptian Pharaoh.

☐   Write an unlikely romance between two historical figures. They do not have to be from the same time period.

☐   The Phonecians dominated sea trade in the 600s BC, sailing as far as Britain and Germany. Write a tale of a Phonecian sailor who is inexplicably stranded in the West after his ship - due to mistake or by design - leaves without him. How does he fare? Does he find a way to return home, or does he build a new life in this foreign land?

☐ Re-imagine today's world with monarchy still intact and functioning as the main system of governance internationally. Set your story in a country of your choosing, minding their given flavor of aristocracy. Have at least one of your main characters be a commoner, and the other a member of the nobility.

☐ Choose an invention, and write about its creator. How did he or she come up with the idea? Why? How have the fruits of their labor changed the world?

☐ Set a story on a Friday 13th, taking into account a specific origin story for the superstition around the day.

☐ Set a story in a historical battle, from the POV of a specific soldier/warrior - either a historical or fictional figure. The battle itself can be one fought in ancient times, or a more modern struggle. Authenticity in terms of describing stakes, terrain, and the like should be a priority. Aim for a pragmatic, no-frills storytelling.

☐ Write a short essay about a fascinating historical figure that is unknown to most people. Tell us the most scandalous of their accomplishments or escapades.

☐   Choose a time period in a particular nation, preferably at least fifty years into the past. Describe a typical day in the life of a person in that time and place.

☐   There are many professions that no longer exist. Select one such profession and write a story set during the height of its popularity. The more ridiculous the job, the better.

Examples include: Lamplighter, town crier, knocker-upper (people hired to knock on windows and wake up others so they could get to work).

☐   Choose a fairy tale. Switch one of the characters with a real historical figure, and retell the story. How would Benjamin Franklin deal with the Big Bad Wolf, as one of the Three Piglets? Would Joan of Arc be as easy to put under a spell as Sleeping Beauty?

☐   Royal weddings were once used as means of forging peace and friendship between nations. Write a story based on one such wedding that has occurred in history.

☐   Write a story in the form of a diary, penned by a historical figure.

☐ A noble woman is preparing for her engagement ball. Focus on the tasks she performs to get ready, with her own feelings about the oncoming nuptials appearing almost secondary. Make sure to establish the time period and country, and keep to the traditions of marriage common at the time.

☐ It was once not so uncommon for a poor family to give away a child to the care of a wealthy, but childless couple. Write about a powerful man who, in his later years, realizes that his real parents are poor commoners. Set the story in a specific country during a particular time, with care to weave the man's position among the country's elite into the plot.

☐ Insert a mythological monster into a time period, and make it a part of history. How does society deal with the monster's emergence? What effect does it have on people's perception of the world? Interweave reality with the supernatural to create an overall uncanny atmosphere.

☐ Set a story in Europe during the Crusades, in a country where people of different religions live together peacefully.

☐   Create a fictional country. Situate it in a time period of your choice, describing its geography, culture, and language. Ensure that it fits in with its neighbors, and that its history is compatible with that of kingdoms and countries nearby.

☐   Take a myth known to sailors - be it of a monster lurking in the depths of the sea, a ghostly ship, or other phenomena - and write a story around it, set in the early 1700s.

☐   Write an adventure tale featuring a real historical figure as its main protagonist. The person you choose can be from any country or time, but must be a woman. The story should be set in the protagonist's own time period.

☐   Imagine the journey of an explorer wandering into uncharted lands.

☐   Explore a historical mystery, such as the disappearance of Amelia Earhart. Invent a plausible explanation of what truly happened.

☐   Set a story during the very beginning of the Dark Ages, at a time when cultural enlightenment is being doused by war and disease.

☐   Choose a historically significant event. Tell a story in which everything is the same, except that the world is ran by highly intelligent cats.

☐   Choose one famous brand of merchandise. Research its history. Write a story about its creator and their initial struggles to get the business off the ground.

☐   A police officer in Edo-period Japan is seeking a troublesome thief. Research police procedures during the time period, with attention to the scenery and local customs.

☐   A soldier falls asleep on the eve of a great battle, only to wake up several decades (or centuries, depending on the story) into the future. Peace reigns between his people and those he had perceived as enemies but a day ago.

☐   Choose one invention important to modern life. Re-imagine contemporary history without that invention's existence.

☐ "Any sufficiently advanced technology is indistinguishable from magic." - Arthur C. Clarke

Use the above quote as inspiration. Does your character invent something incredible in a time when technology is not well understood or widely used, and deemed a witch? Perhaps a time-traveler finds their way to an earlier time period, and dazzles the crowds with modern technology?

☐ Choose a famous speech, preferably one of some age. Annotate the speech with your thoughts and reactions to its contents. Write a reply to the speech, from present-day perspective.

☐ Write a spy story set during the Cold War era. A NATO agent is being pursued by the KGB, in neutral territory. Both the agent and the KGB are trying to keep a low profile. Make the story as realistic as possible.

Note: A large number of once-confidential Cold War era documents have been released to the public. Perusing them may be of interest.

☐ Two warring tribes come together to face an even greater threat to their lands.

☐ Set a story in three different time periods, from ancient to modern. Focus on everyday interactions between people, and the fact that little has changed in that aspect over the centuries.

☐ Write a detective story that solves a real-life, historical mystery. Have your detective figure out the identity of Jack the Ripper as the crimes are being committed, for example. The more obscure the mystery you choose, the better and more interesting for the reader!

☐ Choose a house that belonged to a famous historical figure. Imagine a scene in the life of that famous person, with great detail to the house as the setting.

You could use...

- Abraham Lincoln's house in Springfield, IL
- Buckingham House (now Buckingham Palace), built by John Sheffield, Earl of Mulgrave
- Ernest Hemingway's house in Florida

☐ Set a story in a small town at a time when people managed most of their needs individually, and preferred to trade services rather than receive monetary payment for goods. A rich man, possibly of noble descent, passes through the town. Build the story around the various reactions of the town's residents.

☐ A ship is swept from its course during a storm. It lands in uncharted waters, and eventually comes upon an unfamiliar shore. The captain decides to stop and ask for help. He and his crew are surprised to discover a civilization as advanced as their own populating the newfound land.

Choose two real cultures - one to serve as the crew's own, the other that of the unknown land. Set the tale in the late 1400s, a time period that marks the beginning of the age of exploration.

☐ There have been people revered as seers throughout history. Choose one such figure and research their predictions. Write a story inspired by what you find.

Possible candidates:

- Baba Vanga (Bulgaria)
- Oracle of Delphi (Greece)
- Merlin (British mythology)

☐   Write a short, newspaper article-styled piece discussing the history of a particularly important place in your own town or city.

☐   Set a story in four different time periods, in four different countries. A time traveler from the distant future visits all four sites. Each time, a person contemporary to the given time period notices the traveler and is astonished by their appearance. Write the story from the perspective of these bemused observers.

☐   The pampered son of a rich merchant decides to break away from his father's house and seek his own fortune in a foreign land. Situate the story in the 1500s, with the son traveling much farther than is wise.

☐   Myths of great treasures buried by warriors and pirates span the globe. Select one such myth and trace its history. Write a fictional story featuring the burial of the treasure.

☐   A woman living in a time when her word and thoughts mean little quietly manipulates her husband into achieving prosperity for their family.

☐   The young son of a noble sneaks out of his home to play with the local kids. He hides his identity, and learns much more about life and his own purpose as someone who will grow into power than his tutors could every offer.

☐   Re-imagine your life, had you been born in a different time period and/or country.

 ORROR

Horror is meant to disturb the reader. A good horror story burrows under the skin, never to be forgotten. Scare away sleep with the prompts below!

Warning: Some of the content in this section may not be suitable for young writers.

☐ Horror doesn't need gore or excessive amounts of blood to be scary. Write a tale incorporating something uncanny - a twist of perception, an unexpected revelation, something ordinary turning terrifying.

In need of inspiration? Write about a boy trying to fall asleep. He hears all sorts of noises in the dark, and keeps telling himself that there's nothing out there, that he is safe. Eventually, the boy falls asleep. The story pans outward, revealing that the boy is in a grave and the noises he hears were the footsteps of people walking above ground.

☐ A couple adopts two siblings, a boy and an older girl. The couple is kind and generous, taking great pains to make their children feel at home. The boy and girl are slowly settling in. It doesn't hurt that their new home is a mansion with miles of beautiful property all around.

While playing, the kids discover a doll in one of the mansion's many bedrooms. They take it to their parents, who deny knowledge of the doll's origin. Over the next weeks, the kids find more evidence of children having lived in the mansion, and recently. Their adoptive parents are also acting strange - going out late at night, checking up on the siblings at all times of the day, asking strange questions...

After overhearing a particularly bewildering and heated argument between their parents, the children decide to make a break for it. They run away from home - but is the danger really in the mansion?

☐ Nightmares come to life - literally. Write a story from the point of view of several characters who are trying to figure out what is happening as the people around them die one by one.

☐   Lewis is the kindest, smartest, funniest boy you will ever meet. He loves his friends. He is lonely without them, and Lewis hates being lonely.

Lewis doesn't age. His friends do - they outgrow and forget him. Lewis reminds them he's there. He makes it so his friends don't age anymore, either. And when there's no one left to play, Lewis moves somewhere else and makes new friends.

☐   Moving to a new town is stressful, but Mika is managing. She has an apartment and a job lined up, likes the city, and is overall enthusiastic to start fresh after a nasty parting with her hometown.

That is, until she begins hearing strange noises at night.

Dead bodies start popping up all over town. The wave of death coincides with Mika's arrival; the town's police force is suspicious. So is Mika. Her neighbors seem like nice people, but *someone* is doing *something* strange in the dead of night.

Mika has no one she can trust or turn to for help.

☐   Write a story featuring a character who is terribly disfigured, or otherwise uncommonly unsightly. A series of gruesome murders have law enforcement pounding down your character's door. Your character is innocent. The real killer is everything your protagonist is not: beautiful, beloved, and rich. Their heart is as ugly as they come.

While writing: Focus on descriptions and characterization. Make the crime scenes gritty and disturbing. Make sure to juxtapose the ugliness of the main character and their surroundings with the light and beauty of the killer.

☐   A small mountain town has been cut off from the rest of the world by a terrible blizzard. Phone lines are down, electricity is gone, and the roads are completely inaccessible.

Someone takes advantage of the storm. People are killed off one by one. The killer isn't choosing their victims at random. What is their purpose? Which of the few hundred people living in the town has fallen to blood thirst, and why?

☐   There is another you out there. A mirror image of you, the same every way - except for that terrible smile on their face. You see your double in your dreams. They're always up to something awful.

☐   A man starts seeing someone in the mirror. Something follows him, a shadow caught in reflections and appearing at the edges of pictures.

Write the story from the point of view of someone who notices the man's predicament and tries to help. Twist: The man is actually possessed, and the shadow following him is his body's true soul, trying to wrestle its body back from an evil spirit.

☐   A small party between close friends devolves into telling stupid ghost stories once the bottles have emptied. Having ran out of material, they come up with the bright idea of imagining how they themselves would die, if their death was to be a grisly murder. The following morning, the group wakes up nursing headaches and no recollection whatsoever of the previous night's events.

Well, *almost* all of them wake up. One partygoer is found in the bathroom, very decidedly and brutally dead - in the very same manner she had predicted her own death would occur the night prior.

☐   Jack wakes up with a knife in his hand and a dismembered corpse in his bed.

☐ A house collapses, trapping a man in its foundations. The house has sat abandoned for many years at the edge of a small town. The man is a vagrant; he had been squatting, and no one knows he is there at all. No help is coming. The man knows he is going to die. He lies under the rubble, legs crushed, and tries to keep the panic at bay.

☐ A person loses their humanity little by little, their sense of self and camaraderie with society whittled away by encounters with terrible people. They become a different type of monster than that found in fairy tales.

☐ Tessa's mother has warned her to never, ever open the door to strangers. But the person knocking is not a stranger. Tessa has known them ever since she can remember - even if only in her nightmares.

☐ A journalist infiltrates a notorious cult, meaning to expose the cult's leader for fraud and the abuse of his followers. The mission slips farther from mind the longer the journalist remains in the cult.

Subgenre: psychological horror

☐ Ryan's only friend is the stranger that lives in the mirror in his bedroom. The man has always been there, growing up with Ryan from a child into an adult. Ryan shares everything with him, as one would with a beloved sibling.

One day, Ryan doesn't go to school. His homeroom teacher contacts Ryan's family, thinking the boy truant. They find Ryan's body in his bedroom, crumpled in front of the broken mirror.

The spirit of the mirror didn't murder the boy. However, Ryan's death had the unexpected effect of acting as a sacrifice and setting the spirit free. It now seeks vengeance on the boy's behalf.

☐ Let's mix some humor in! Write a typical horror story following a main character who fears none of its events. People are killed left and right, terrifying demons stalk the protagonist and his/her crew, what have you - and the MC remains absolutely unmoved. He/she ridicules every scary situation instead.

Your choice in how the tale ends - whether with evil's defeat, or the MC's death. Do make it funny!

☐   A brutal murder leaves a family without a father. The distraught mother seeks the support of a neighboring family as she navigates the chaotic aftermath of the case.

The neighbors have a young daughter. She is not at all happy with having the bereft family over every other day. Mostly because she is convinced that the woman's two young children are behind their father's murder.

☐   The ghost of a young girl is not the scariest thing living in the Johnson's house. She tries to warn visitors, but always, always fails.

☐   "They are not my parents," the child says.

☐   A man-eating deity awakens.

☐   A man finds a letter in his home. It seems as if it was written by someone who knows him very well. The letter warns that the man himself is about to do something terrible. The man is befuddled - he is not the kind of person to do anything criminal. He throws the letter out, but can't seem to dismiss it from his thoughts.

☐   A group of strangers is forced together in a cabin in the middle of the woods, seeking shelter from a sudden storm. All have arrived separately - some by car, others caught by the bad weather while hiking. Yet nature and accident has brought them under one roof.

Or so it appears.

Something prowls around the cabin. Something has brought each of the people inside to this precise spot, and trapped them there. Blood will run before the mystery is solved.

☐   A man's life is crumbling before his eyes. His misfortune is the doing of someone very close to him - a fact the man doesn't realize until it is much too late to reach out to anyone else for help.

☐   A woman who has been in a coma for several months wakes up one morning, healthy and aware. She is signed out of the hospital that very day, to the delight of her family.

However, the woman going home is not the same person who had went into the hospital. Or rather, she is not a person at all. Something much more sinister has made itself at home in the woman's vacant body.

☐ Someone has gotten a hold of Becky's phone number. She begins to receive strange messages at all times of day and night. Most are single words. Others are entire paragraphs that make no sense. Becky replies at times, when she is bored.

Then the pictures start to come, and Becky finally understands she is dealing with someone terribly dangerous.

☐ There are some family secrets that should never be unearthed. Kyle discovers this the hard way.

☐ A witch steals eyes in exchange for wishes. Each wish the witch grants twists into something terrible.

☐ People close to Irene Miller begin to die, suddenly and without any apparent cause. The police suspects ill intent in a few cases, but most seem to be either natural or accidental. Irene - a closeted believer in the supernatural - thinks something otherworldly is involved.

In reality, the killer is quite human. They are aware of Irene's obsession with the occult, and are styling the murders for her benefit.

☐   A serial killer targets people only on Halloween. They dress in different costumes every year and dispose of their victims by putting up their bodies as Halloween decorations in the yards of random homes.

This year, the killer makes a mistake. They target a retired detective, and find themselves the prey rather than the predator.

☐   The owner of a small flower shop receives an order for four red roses on the first of every month. They don't think anything of it, until the police issues a public notice of a serial killer who leaves a bouquet of four red roses on their victims' bodies. The shop owner is convinced that their repeat customer is the killer. Their suspicions only grow when a perusal of the sales log reveals that each order, although identical, had been purchased under a different name.

The shop owner attempts to trace the means of payment to the buyer. This alerts the killer to the unwanted attention.

☐   Living a normal life is impossible when monsters dog your every step. Monsters no one ever sees, not until they've gotten their claws in someone's heart and poisoned their mind.

☐ A renowned wig-maker is sought the world-over for his artistic touch. The wigs the man makes are one of a kind. They are all natural, human hair - although the manner of the hair's acquirement is anything but ordinary.

☐ Something evil haunts a woman's house. It makes its presence felt in strange ways, but doesn't harm its human host - the creature needs the woman in order to continue existing. Visitors are not as fortunate.

The creature doesn't kill people. It twists their minds and fills them with evil.

☐ A serial killer leaves poems as calling cards. Each poem is particular to the victim, and contains a clue to the killer's own identity. With every case, it becomes more and more obvious that the killer may in fact be a law enforcement officer of some kind. The FBI agents working on the case begin to jump at shadows, suspecting everyone - including each other.

☐ After a week of sleepless nights, a man starts seeing strange things everywhere he goes. He assumes the cause to be sleep-deprivation. He is half-right; his muddled state allows him to perceive things he would usually not be able to see - horrible things that are very much real.

☐   Write a short tale featuring your favorite horror villain. The story in question doesn't have to fall squarely into the horror genre. Have fun with it, and the character! Crossovers with other fictional works are welcomed.

☐   A character goes on a murdering spree. Tell the story from the killer's perspective, while being careful not to make the protagonist sympathetic to the reader. Have your audience ride along with the main character, feeling repulsed yet powerless - not unlike the killer's victims.

☐   An old woman sits on a bench in front of a house. She is murmuring names to herself while knitting.

The names belong to people living in the house. The woman is a stranger to them. The names she speaks as she knits are of lives that will soon be lost.

☐   Bad thoughts crawl out of people's heads and turn into tiny shadows that coalesce into a single creature. The more bad thoughts a person has, the bigger the monsters grow, until they take the shape of the person who had spawned them and wreck havoc wearing their face.

[ ]   After watching a horror movie about black magic and witchery, a group of kids have some fun by play-cursing a few of their classmates. They make up spells and a silly ritual, and giggle about it all night.

Unfortunately for their classmates, one of the kids happens to come from a line of witches. The spells hold, and the curses come true.

[ ]   A famous actor is also an infamous killer. A no-name actor makes the link between the two personas, but needs hard proof to get the man in the police's radar. This involves gaining the killer's confidence. But is the killer really unaware of the wannabe hero's intentions?

[ ]   It is a slow, hot, humid day. A man sits in a chair. He is tied, blindfolded, and gagged. Sweat mats his hair and sticks his clothes to his skin. He strains to hear something, anything, but the world is dead quiet.

A door opens. Someone walks in, their steps as loud as gunshots.

[ ]   A crew of astronauts arrives back on Earth. They find death and destruction, and no explanation for what had occurred - and no one left to ask.

☐ A young man is convinced the woman in the apartment next door is watching him while he is in his apartment. The smiles she gives him when they cross paths make him shake. Late at night, he lays awake, waiting for the door to his bedroom to creak open.

Is the man going out of his mind, or is there something to his worries? Write the story with an untrustworthy narrator in the young man.

☐ A diner serves coffee laced with poison to one unlucky customer each month. The customer in question dies exactly 48 hours later, with an audience of one - the person responsible for the poisonous drink.

☐ Samantha doesn't take the recent break-up with her long-time boyfriend well. She drives to his house one late, sleepless night, and bears witness to something that wipes all lovelorn thoughts from her head.

☐ There is a strange package under the tree on Christmas morning that no one remembers wrapping. It is addressed to the entire family, and it appears to be...moving.

☐ A man programs others to kill for him using hypnosis. Anyone he meets can be turned into a murderer - or become a victim.

☐ Pick an ordinary household item. Make it a source of horror, so much so that the reader will have trouble keeping it in their house after reading your story.

☐ Murals depicting people playing out various scenes from Greek tragedies begin to appear around a large city. The murals are realistic, cast so the figures of people and animals pop out of the wall.

A passerby happens to lean against one of the murals - and feels a heartbeat.

☐ A woman lures children to her home, and feeds them to death.

 **OURNAL**

Keeping a journal is a fun, relaxing way to stretch your writing muscles. The prompts in this section will have you grabbing for a pen in delight. Happy writing!

☐　　Choose one simple thing you did today. Write about the experience in minute detail, including people you met, objects you touched, and things you saw. Aim for at least 500 words.

☐　　Write about a personal failure that seemed soul-crushing at the time, but proved all for the better in retrospect.

☐　　Describe your dream vacation. Where would you go? What sights would you visit while you're there?

☐   Make a list of rights you believe every human being should have. Feel free to expand on particular entries, i.e. provide your reasoning.

Example: In his article, "Conjuring New Human Rights," law scholar and human rights advocate Philip Alston listed some unusual rights for consideration, including: "The right to sleep;" "The right to coexist with nature;" and, "The right not to be exposed to excessively and unnecessarily heavy, degrading, dirty, and boring work" (1984, p. 610).

☐   Retell something that happened to you from the point of view of someone else who was there.

☐   List all the small things that make you happy during the day.

Samples from our own list:

- Espresso in the morning
- Crisp air
- Sunlight slanting through the windows
- A cat stalking across the lawn

☐ Write out a grocery list of items you need for the house, recording each as a silly sentence.

Ex.: Shower curtains shouldn't blow into the tub, that's not how sailing works.

☐ How do you "waste time?" Make a list of the not-so-productive ways you spend your free time. Explain why you enjoy the particular activity.

☐ Write down at least one thing you did today that you would like to remember ten years from now.

☐ What kind of world would you have, if you could reshape it to your liking? Think specific, and remember that ideals are all good and lovely, but they don't mean anything if they can't be realized.

☐ Write a short story featuring one of your personal, silly quirks.

☐ If you could give one advice to a future generation, an advice hard-won through your own experiences, what would it be?

☐ Describe a tradition shared in your family, or within your friend group. It can have religious or cultural roots. Talk about its significance and why it is important to you.

If no suitable traditions come to mind, make up a new one and tell us all about it!

☐ Have you ever been lost? Write about one such instance. Recall how you felt the moment you realized that you didn't know where you were, and how you resolved the entire situation. Did you learn anything from the experience?

☐ Who was the last person you talked to today? Describe your relationship with them, including how you met and their significance to you.

☐ Take note of your immediate surroundings. What kind of trees grow near your home? Flowers? Is the ground flat or uneven, grassy or cement? Note down colors, textures, smells - anything and everything you notice.

☐ Is there something you would never, ever do again? Write about the experience. Word the essay as if you're trying to convince someone who is in a similar situation not to do what you had done. The subject can be as silly or as serious as you would like.

☐ Is there something you would love to do, but are too scared to try? What about things you do often/daily, but would rather never do again? Why?

☐ List ten books you believe everyone should read. Try to explain why in a single sentence per book.

☐ What do you think birds talk about? Write a short dialogue between two birds, be it wild or tamed.

☐ Make a list of jokes you like. Try to add a few of your own creation.

☐ Doodle a short comic strip. It should be a complete scene, telling a story. Limit the accompanying dialogue and descriptions to the space available in the thought and speech bubbles around the characters' heads.

☐ What is the clearest memory you have of your childhood? Why do you remember that precise moment? Depict the memory in a story, making it as detailed as possible.

☐   Nitpick a novel you like, listing plot-holes, unbelievable twists, out-of-character moments - anything and everything that stood out to you as a reader.

☐   Draw yourself as a superhero, or a princess, or a mythological creature - something you would have drawn as a child. Write a short story to go along with the drawing. Have fun!

☐   Is there a day in your life you would like to repeat - either to change something, or simply relive the experience again? Which day is it? What happened? What makes it special?

☐   Pretend you live in modern China, or Victorian-era Europe, or any place and time you like. What would your daily thoughts, routines, and worries be? What would you put down in your journal?

☐   Are there any names you find particularly appealing? Some you absolutely hate? Note down your reasons.

☐   What would you love to receive as a gift? Make a list, featuring both the present in question and the person from whom you would like to receive the specific gift.

☐ Are there any extraordinary individuals in your family tree? Any stories about distant relatives that have been passed down generations? Note down a noteworthy tale you have heard about a family member, or otherwise create one about you that you would like generations from now to remember.

☐ What is the silliest thing you have done to get someone's attention? Did it work?

☐ It is a dark, stormy afternoon. The skies are black, the trees rustle and creak, and the windows drum with rain. You have the day free. What are you up to?

☐ How would a stranger describe you, after a brief meeting?

☐ List ten significant events that have happened to you in the last ten years of your life. If possible, list one event per year.

☐ Are there any songs you know by heart? Any associations with a particular piece of music - perhaps a cherished memory, or an important occasion?

☐ Choose a few locations around your home, at random. Set a short story in each, with particular attention to the physical characteristics of the scene.

☐ Make a list of childhood friends with whom you have fallen out of touch. Write down the clearest memory you have of each person on the list.

☐ There are places that change us. Write of an experience tied to a specific place that has impacted your life in a significant way.

☐ Create a family tree for your own family. Try to go as far back as you can. If possible, include a snippet of a story for each person.

☐ List books and/or movies you have read/seen, and found so terrible they are funny. Write a short, humorously dramatic description for each entry.

☐ We change as we age - or rather, we become more ourselves. How have you changed from your childhood? Your teens? Are there any major alterations in how you view yourself now as opposed to back then?

☐   What was your favorite fairy tale as a child? Write your own version of the story, meant for an adult audience.

☐   What was the worst job you ever had? Write a short story with your hated workplace as the setting.

☐   Write down a secret you have kept for years, either your own or one entrusted to you by someone else.

☐   Make a list of things you would do if you suddenly become immensely rich.

☐   Write a story featuring a proverb of your own creation.

☐   Write down a short description of every interaction you have with a stranger during your day, whether brief or lengthy. Do this for at least a week. At the end of the week, select one of the people you met and write a story featuring a character modeled after them.

☐   Tell of your day as if it was experienced by someone else and only recorded by you, an impartial observer.

☐ The flow of time hits an unexpected snag, causing everyone and everything to fall still. You are the only one unaffected. What do you do? Assume that this is a temporary situation, and that no one is in any danger.

☐ What quirks and habits have you inherited from your family? Make a list.

☐ Write about five important moments in your life: one funny; one sweet; one sad; one scary; and one surprising.

☐ If you could change the name your parents gave you at birth, what name would you choose for yourself? Why?

☐ Your dearest wish has come true. What was it? How has your life changed as a result?

☐ Do one thing you have never done before every day, for five days. Describe each experience in writing.

☐ You have been asked to give a speech at the graduation ceremony of your old high school. Write that speech.

AGICAL REALISM

Magical realism is a genre in which the supernatural coexists with the ordinary, surprising the reader with outlandish tales set in the most common of places. The prompts below will have you finding magic everywhere you look!

☐   A girl with a mirror for a face arrives in a small, sleepy town.

☐   The world is the same as we know it now, but every living creature has a double who is their exact spiritual opposite - in mannerism, thoughts, and personality - somewhere on Earth. Write about a meeting between two people who are each other's "other self."

☐   People can be only wholly good, or wholly evil. Traumatic events can flip a person from one side of the coin to the other, but there is no gray area in between. Write about such a world, creating a story based in a society in which good and evil people coexist.

☐ A boy finds a large, glass marble painted to look like a disembodied eye. When the boy picks it up, the marble jumps into his face. Plop! The boy's left eye falls out, turning into a marble. The glass eye is now a real eye. The boy blinks. The world looks strange.

What does the boy see with his new eye?

☐ There are two humanoid species on Earth: humans, and humanoid mammals - that is, humans with animal features. The two are perfectly aware of each other and live mostly in peace. That doesn't mean strange situations don't arise when they are forced in close quarters.

Such as rooming together in college.

☐ A woman and a mermaid share an apartment. Or rather, a bathtub.

It's not the worst living arrangement in the building - the guy in 3A has to deal with a dragon hoarding his socks.

☐ Everyone has magic. Little children get tiny dragons as pets, chase fairies and gnomes in their parents' gardens, and dance with the elven folk.

Set a normal, everyday scene in such a world.

☐ Strong emotions cause physical changes to people's appearances.

> *The classics*: jealousy turns one's face green
> *Quirky*: happiness makes one's hair curly

☐ On nights the moon shines full, water touched by moonlight becomes a door to a different realm. Strange, beautiful creatures make their way through to walk among humans.

☐ Minor sicknesses appear as physical changes of a supernatural kind. Rashes show up as scales; sneezing due to allergy results in breathing fire or setting off minor earthquakes - that sort of thing.

☐ Everything is the same as it is now, except animals can talk like humans and in the languages of whatever country they reside. Cue snotty cats with international passports, speaking English with French accents.

☐ People are born with animal companions, who are manifestations of their souls. They are not always visible to others, but are inseparable from their given person.

☐ People born with witch eyes can see supernatural creatures. Many try to hide their gift, knowing that they will be forced into service guarding the border between the human and the supernatural realms.

☐ Shadows have personalities. They speak to each other just as humans do, have friends and enemies, and prefer certain things over others. Tell a story of an extremely introverted individual with a party-animal of a shadow.

☐ Magic is real, and studied as a science. No one who practices magic becomes particularly powerful - it's not the sort of magic seen in fantastic tales, but a theoretical academic field with some practical applications.

An entrepreneur utilizes their MAD (Magic Academy Degree) to create a line of teas that enhance one of the drinker's senses for a brief period after consumption. One of the blends proves faulty. The side-effects are hilarious.

☐ Animals can talk. Humanity understands them. Having pets is more like having roommates who don't pay rent.

☐   Being dead isn't all it is hyped up to be. The dead society is just as monotonous as that of the living, except it goes on *forever*.

The living are somewhat aware of what awaits them after death. Mostly due to the fact that deadmen employed as Messengers flit between the living and dead worlds, delivering goodness knows what and to whom.

☐   Tree spirits are notorious for being pranksters. They giggle creepily at night, pelt passersby with acorns and cones, and generally make themselves a nuisance.

Tell a tale of a tree spirit messing with nearby humans.

☐   The earth spins backwards every million years or so. When it does, strange things happen to the creatures living on its surface.

A million years from the last counter-spin, the Earth is getting ready to turn back again. The threads of time and reality are about to bend out of shape.

☐   In a world where a wish can come true if wanted badly enough, wishing for things in the heat of the moment can end up poorly indeed.

☐   The skies rain various things: water, flowers, chocolate... Umbrellas are simply not cutting it anymore.

☐   Celestial beings land on Earth sometimes. Each is unique, from their size - some are as tall as mountains, others as tiny as ants - to their features. However, all share a certain disregard for humans. The beings walk around, careful not to stomp on someone (or be stomped on), but don't try to interact with any earthly creature.

☐   People possess elemental affinities; water, earth, air, or fire. Some are more powerful than others. Then there is Jo, who has no affinity toward anything at all, elemental or otherwise. Jo's extreme apathy is in fact her own special power - the ability to "dampen" other people's talents, lessening their effect.

     Someone not very nice takes an interest in Jo and her quirky ability.

☐   A little girl plays with her neighbor, who happens to be a fox kit in human guise.

☐ The people of Earth and the people of the Sky come into contact once every hundred years, when heaven and earth come together for the span of a single month. During that time, it is possible to cross from one realm to the other. But those who do must be careful to cross back in time, as the two realms will pull apart again and not come together in a human lifetime.

A girl from Earth doesn't make the deadline. She is trapped in the heavenly realm, but determined to find a way back home.

☐ Whales walk on land, and humans live under the sea.

☐ Being the only magical creature in an all-human high school is tough. What's tougher? Failing to meet your classmates' silly expectations of your species.

☐ Trees can speak. The older they are, the wiser they think themselves to be, resulting in lots of unwanted advice offered to humans passing under their branches.

☐ The world is the same, except cats have evolved into humanoid beings in the stead of homo-sapiens. One such cat falls through a world-wrap, and ends up on human-dominated Earth.

☐   Some people are born with the Evil Eye. Their jealousy, hatred, or fear can plague others as sickness. All it takes is a single glance.

☐   The world is made up of sets of identical twins. Each person has a visual double walking around, and they are always the exact opposite in terms of personality. The catch? One of the twins is always invisible to everyone but their sibling.

☐   Ancient civilizations believed that if the memory of a person exists, they will live on beyond death. Set a story in a world where this belief holds true.

☐   A witch spells the water source of a small town. The people in the town grow animal ears and tails, matching the animal closest to their individual personalities. Traits associates with their animal alter egos are also exaggerated.

☐   The invention of DreamCatchers - technology that can detect and "catch" nightmares - makes sleeping an infinitely more pleasant experience. Unfortunately, malfunctions have been known to happen. One such traps a nervous sleeper in their worst nightmare.

☐ A man falls in love with his male best friend. As his friend is heterosexual, the man resigns himself to suffering from unrequited love for the rest of his life.

That is, until a wizard offers to turn him into a woman.

Does the man take the offer? If he does, does his becoming a woman make a difference in his relationship with his friend?

☐ Kate turns into a cat sometimes.

It's no big deal, really. Though it would be better if she could actually control where and when the transformations take place. As is, she is prone to getting herself into embarrassing situations.

☐ A witch moves next door to a family with two teenage kids. The teens complain of boredom constantly, and are as whiny and dramatic as befitting of their age group. The witch decides to help spice up their lives.

☐ Life and death are a closed circle. When the body dies, the essence of a person slips into a new host, and is reborn. The memory of the previous life does not make the journey - or at least, not usually.

☐ A new drug has hit the streets. It has people hallucinating strange creatures and abusing 911 with calls about supernatural happenings. Analysis of the drug in question leaves scientists baffled. The substance cannot be identified, as its contents seem to keep shifting. What is more interesting, none of them are chemicals known to mankind.

☐ Set a story in a universe where animals are humanoid, magical, and keep humans as pets rather than the other way around.

☐ A party-wizard comes into possession of a real magic hat. The things he pulls out of it are definitely stranger than bunnies.

☐ People are born with half a soul. The other half is hidden somewhere in the world, and must be found in order for a person to be truly happy.

☐ Pets gain the ability of human speech. It's less exciting a phenomenon than one may think, given most animals' rather limited range of interests. Cats, naturally, turn to blackmail almost immediately.

☐   Cooking is an act of magic. Eating food prepared with love makes one happy and healthy. The opposite is true of food made out of spite, or by someone hateful.

☐   Wishing trees exist. Wishes made beneath their branches are caught in their leaves and woven into a song, carried to the heavens by the wind.

☐   A tiny, humanoid species of plant people lives in human gardens.

☐   Once per year in the depths of winter, a parade made up of masked creatures passes through a small human town. The parade makes for a grand sight, and draws huge crowds of tourists. Approaching the parade is however never wise.

☐   All superstitions are true. Breaking them carries very real consequences.

☐   Carving a mouth or eyes into an inanimate object grants the item the ability of speech or sight for a limited amount of time.

☐   People can change their scent to entice or repel others. Perfumes are used to mask such natural scents, or protect against their misuse.

☐   Electricity is harvested from the skies, and produced by a deity or another supernatural being.

☐   Some people are born with clocks in their chests, where a heart ought to be. They are able to stop, reverse, or speed up reality, moving through time as one would through water.

 YSTERY/THRILLER

Thrilling tales of twisty mysteries will keep a reader glued to the page - and are a great fun to write, besides! Find your inspiration in the prompts below.

☐ Rena Andrews is informed that she is adopted. She is 24 and has just been kidnapped. The piece of news had been kindly delivered by her abductors. The thugs are talking about mob wars and mafia dons, and acting strangely deferential. Rena is certain they'd gotten the wrong person. Until she actually meets her supposed father, and things just... click.

As do a lot of guns.

☐ An egg the size of an adult human appears in your character's garden. Is it a prank? Some sort of tech a government plane dropped by mistake?

Well, whatever it is, it's hatching.

☐ Daryl feels eyes on him whenever he is outside. He calls himself paranoid and laughs off the possibility of having a stalker. The unease at the pit of his stomach grows and grows.

Daryl is right to be concerned - but not for himself. The person being followed is in fact Daryl's next-door neighbor and colleague at work. In undertaking to find his stalker, Daryl involves himself in someone else's nightmare.

☐ Your character wakes up in the middle of the night. He/she hears a strange noise - it sounds as if someone else is in the room.

Write a story around that moment: Moving from sleep, to confusion, to panic, all in the span of a few minutes. Is there someone else in the room? Do they mean your character harm? You can let the audience know, or leave us hanging.

☐ A family goes missing, one by one. A detective is working feverishly to figure out who is behind the kidnappings, where they are taking the victims, and why the remaining family members don't seem concerned.

☐   A woman receives a text from someone she doesn't know. It appears to be sent by mistake. The woman means to tell the sender so, but she's at work and an urgent project has her forgetting about her phone. She is surprised to find over a dozen messages when she gets home. The texts go from strange to morbid very quickly.

The woman realizes that the person who was supposed to receive the messages is in great danger. She calls the police, but there isn't much information she can give them. Something about the texts is bothering her... the wording is extraordinarily familiar.

The sender is someone from the woman's workplace. But who? And who is their target?

☐   Write a murder-house mystery. The usual set-up: fancy party at a remote manor, the owner of the house is murdered, the killer cuts power/hi-jinks transport and leaves the guests trapped. Build the suspense around the reveal of the killer. Is it one of the guests? Someone on the victim's staff? A third party?

☐   A simple robbery takes a dark turn when the would-be thieves discover something sinister in their target's house.

Worse yet, the master of the home has just returned, and he knows his secret has been discovered.

☐ A novelist works from home. When the empty apartment above hers gets rented out, she finds her peaceful work routine interrupted by loud neighbors. On a particularly noisy day, with a deadline looming, she finally gathers the courage to go yell at the people upstairs. A young man opens the door. He apologizes, promising that he and his roommate will keep it down in the future.

A few days later, the novelist hears loud thumping from upstairs that doesn't stop for some time. She goes to visit her neighbors again, partially out of concern. A middle-aged woman opens the door. She apologizes to the novelist. There is no sign of the young man or his roommate.

The days that follow are very, very quiet. The novelist is certain something is wrong.

☐ A man finds out that his girlfriend of two years has been lying to him about...everything. Her job, her family, even her nationality, for Pete's sake! What the man doesn't know is *why*. She isn't getting anything out of the deal, other than him - and she's always had him. The lies were never necessary.

The man keeps quiet about his newfound knowledge. He starts stalking his girlfriend, trying to figure out what she has been up to. He quickly realizes that he has bitten more than he can chew.

☐   A man starts hearing a strange, rasping sound coming from the ceiling. He lives alone in an old country house passed down in his family. The roof of the house is pointed and hollow. There is no proper room above the ceiling of the second story, just empty, flat space that had once been used to store food come winter.

The noise always comes at night. Fed up, the man decides to investigate. He guesses some sort of animal has made the roof its den.

The man doesn't find an animal. Or rather, not quite.

☐   Daily life involves routines. Commuting to work leads to familiarity with the "regulars" who ride the bus at the same time as you every day. It's not uncommon.

What is strange is seeing the same woman every time you board a bus, be it weekday or weekend, whether you're running late or going in early. She watches you when she thinks you can't see her. You are curious and very much unsettled.

One day, tired after a long shift at work and fed up with being stared at by some strange woman, you decide to approach her.

Here is where the story turns for the weird and very much worse.

☐   A suburban neighborhood finds itself plagued by the strangest nuisance: unidentified knocking late at night. It happens to one house per night, and over the course of several months, no house has been left undisturbed. The identity of the late-night visitor remains a mystery.

Until tonight.

☐   An unsigned letter is delivered to the residence of a woman who has recently lost her husband to an accident. The letter holds that the death was a murder. The woman is terrified.

She is the one who had arranged for her husband's death.

The letter's sender doesn't appear to know who the killer is, but has cause to suspect a murder. Write the tale from the widow's perspective as she tries to figure out who the sender is and what she is to do about this unfortunate snag in her plans.

☐   Write a locked-room murder mystery, with a twist - none of the people suspected had actually 'dun' the deed.

☐ Pet dogs and cats begin disappearing. It is a city-wide phenomenon that prompts a serious police response and a lot of media attention. People expect some sort of strange, organized crime ring to be behind the pet-nappings. No ransom has been demanded, however. What is more, a few of the missing pets are eventually discovered wandering in neighboring cities. They seem to be leaving voluntarily.

Conspiracy theories about aliens, oncoming natural disasters, and the like quickly proliferate. One of them is in fact correct. It's up to the protagonists to figure out which one, before it is too late.

☐ Raul starts to lose time. It's minutes at first, then hours, and now he can't remember entire days. He is afraid that something is wrong with him, but can't bring himself to share what is happening with anyone or go to a doctor. Raul starts to suspect that someone is playing a really cruel trick on him. He grows more and more paranoid, especially around a certain someone who has been out to get him ever since Raul took over his family's company.

Are Raul's fears founded, or is he truly losing his grip on reality?

☐ A man receives a number of small gifts over the course of several weeks. A gift arrives every Wednesday, to his home, with no note or sender's address attached. The gifts themselves are...strange, to say the least. The man wonders whose attention he has caught, and why. The missives hardly seem like a courting gesture, but what else can they be?

☐ A journalist suspects a small local restaurant to be a front for a money laundering operation. She/he stakes out the place, becoming a regular customer. The journalist slowly comes to enjoy the company of the restaurant's owners. However, her/his intuition is not wrong - there is something not so legal going on in the place. Worse, it seems the owners' involvement is forced. But why are they cooperating? What goods are being delivered to the restaurant on monthly basis, but never leaving the premises?

☐ Noa makes friends with a strange creature living in a nearby forest. The creature seems friendly enough where Noa is concerned. To other people, however, the creature is a danger of the worst kind. Is Noa special, or as damned as the creature itself?

☐   A girl dreams of someone she has never met. She dreams of this person night after night after night, until they are all that she can think about, even when awake.

☐   Write a murder mystery from the killer's perspective. The crime has already been committed, and the investigation is underway. The killer is playing with the police, amusing him/herself by keeping close and monitoring the situation.

☐   Numbers are chalked onto the front doors of every house in an affluent suburban neighborhood. The chalk is easy enough to scrub off, and the occurrence is dismissed as a stupid prank.

Until a new number appears on every door.

The numbers change every day, regardless of whether the house's owners bother to remove the chalk or let it sit. It doesn't take long for people to figure out that they are marking a countdown - each morning, the number is one less than what it had been the night prior.

But a countdown to what?

☐   There is someone in Sandy's basement. She can hear them moving in the dead of night, and while she can't find a trace of anyone during the day, no one can convince her that she is alone in her home.

☐ A teenager runs away from home - or so everyone seems to believe. Everyone, that is, except the teen's father. The man is convinced something has happened to his child, that she/he has not left the family voluntarily. He is determined to uncover the truth.

☐ A woman hears her window creaking late at night. The sound startles her out of sleep; she finds nothing out of the ordinary in her room. The sound repeats every night for a week. The woman grows more and more frightened, yet nothing ever happens.

Then one night, the sound doesn't come.

In the morning, the woman is gone.

☐ A petty thief trying to make a name for himself happens to decide on a calling card similar to the one used by a dangerous criminal sought by the FBI. The thief is horrified when news of murders start flooding the news, reported as connected to the few heists he'd managed to pull off. He decides to find the killer, and clear his name.

The thief is not the only one angry at having his trademark stolen. The killer is looking for the punk impersonating his calling card, as well.

☐   Sherry is obsessed with mystery books. She has read most everything in the genre - which is why she recognizes a slew of recent crimes as identical to those that occur in a little-known series of mystery novels.

☐   Sergej is adopted. He has been looking for his real parents for years - not because he is unhappy with his adoptive family, but so he can figure out the reason he sees the world so differently than everyone around him.

In the end, Sergej's blood family finds him rather than the other way around. That is not a good thing.

☐   Debbie Carlson has been dead for years. Her killer has assumed her identity and built a new life for herself.

When a relative the killer was unaware Debbie had shows up, the killer scrambles to cover her tracks and protect everything she has built under Debbie's name.

☐   The sole heir of a wealthy family is found dead in his bedroom. He has obviously been murdered, but no motive seems apparent - the man had no lovers, owed no one anything, and had no heirs of his own who stood to inherit his fortune.

The case grows more befuddling when the man's body disappears from the morgue.

☐ Someone is buying off properties in a small, provincial town. One of the remaining residents - an elderly woman - refuses to sell her home to the mysterious buyer. Her untimely death shocks the town, and brings the woman's granddaughter to investigate.

☐ Two men find a pot of gold while working a rich man's fields. The gold likely belongs to their employer's family, buried for safe-keeping decades ago and forgotten. The men split the gold and make a pact to never utter a word about it to anyone.

Neither man trusts the other will keep his word.

☐ Millie Simmons' murder shakes a small town. Her killer is never found, and the case remains a mystery. Two decades later, a special news report on Millie reawakens public interest in the case. Private detectives descend on the city, hoping to find the killer and capitalize on the resulting media attention.

When one of the detectives is killed in a way similar to Millie Simmons' murder of twenty years prior, the stakes of the game go way up.

☐ Lorie's mother disappears, leaving behind a cryptic note as the first of a series of clues for her daughter. They do not point to the missing woman's whereabouts, but guide Lorie along a quest to solve a great mystery that has been plaguing her hometown for decades.

☐ Sasha lives in a large apartment complex. The apartment directly below him is occupied by an elderly woman who lives alone and appears to have no family. Sasha visits her several times a week, to make sure she doesn't need anything and because he genuinely enjoys her company.

One rainy Sunday, he rings the bell only to have a complete stranger open the door. A confused back-and-forth follows; the woman Sasha had befriended appears to have moved. According to the stranger, she had done so several weeks ago - something Sasha knows to be a lie.

☐ A hotel burns down to the ground. Several people die in the fire, including the hotel's owner. One of the surviving guests is convinced that the fire had not been accidental.

☐ The priest serving a small rural town is found dead. The death itself appears natural, and there are no signs of struggle. However, the fact that the three previous priests assigned to the town had died under similar circumstances does give the local police force a cause for concern.

☐ A person disappears every year from a small town. The disappearances always occur on the same day, and no trace of the person missing is ever found.

Until a high school girl manages to scribble a message before she is spirited away.

☐ Sam takes a job as part-time security guard at a local cemetery. The job is easy - the cemetery is closed to visitors at night, and only a few of the church staff are ever around. Sam begins to wonder why the job even exists.

That is, until someone breaks into the cemetery and desecrates a grave in a most troubling fashion.

Sam doesn't see the perpetrator. In a panic over losing his job, he hides the evidence of the break-in and fixes the grave as best as he can. The following night, he throws in a few extra patrols around the grounds and watches the security cameras like a hawk. In the morning, he finds a second grave has been defaced. There is a message scrawled over the headstone, too - and it calls Sam out by name.

☐ A famous detective has a secret. His apparent genius is in fact borrowed from his wife, whose detective skills are unmatched but impossible to advertise in their stuffy Victorian society.

The detective's wife goes missing while investigating a case. The detective struggles to piece the clues of her disappearance together.

☐ A young child is left an orphan after her family's murder. The motive behind the killings is unclear, since nothing was stolen from the family's home and no one save the family's children stood to benefit from the deaths. The parents co-owned a multi-million dollar company, which will now go to their daughter once she reaches majority.

The police has no suspects in custody. Most are rather baffled about the girl's survival, as she had been in the house at the time of the murders. Unsavory gossip begins to spread.

The young girl is certainly involved, but not in the manner the yellow papers suggest. She holds the key for busting the case wide open - a key she takes with her when she runs away from protective custody and disappears.

☐ A pick-pocket is sifting through the day's loot when she/he comes upon a strange item - a large, gold pocket watch. The watch seems faintly familiar. The thief learns why when a story about the death of a renowned CEO repeats on the evening news. Apparently, all has been accounted for on the man's body except the gold pocket watch that is now in the thief's possession.

The thief fights with his/her conscience about taking the watch to the police.

☐ A small, family-owned crafts store finds itself in the spotlight when a notorious serial killer leaves one of their signature products at the scene of the latest murder. The store has no camera surveillance. The piece is one of half a dozen made, so the pool of suspects is not too large.

More worrying - the store's clients are all people the owners know and trust. A killer seems to be hiding among the familiar faces.

☐ The sky above a certain city turns red. The surrounding area is unaffected, and no natural cause seems apparent.

☐   A police officer questions a woman regarding a murder that has taken place in an upscale apartment building. The woman hasn't actually seen anything, and tells the officer so. The officer takes the woman's statement and leaves.

A few minutes later, two officers corner the woman to question her about the very same murder. The woman tells them that someone had already taken her statement. The officers leave in a hurry, believing that the murderer had impersonated a police officer and is even now covering his tracks.

The fake officer is not caught. The next day, the same two officers return to the apartment building, wanting to ask the woman more questions regarding the case and the man who had originally taken her statement. The woman doesn't answer her door. The officers find the building's superintendent and ask him to open the woman's apartment. The man goes along, but voices his confusion - no one has lived in that apartment for over a year.

Who is the real killer?

☐ Michael's ex-girlfriend is harassing him online and over his phone. He finally has enough, and goes to confront her. He finds her apartment empty. Undeterred, Michael goes to visit her mother - and learns that his ex had died in a car crash shortly after their break-up.

☐ Elizabeth has twelve sisters. They share an eerie beauty that Elizabeth lacks, and often speak in riddles. Elizabeth has no parents; her sisters raise her, alone in a house far up a steep mountain. Sometimes, they take her down to the city below - always late at night, when the moon is high in the sky. Elizabeth doesn't like going there. She always gets lost in the crowd, wandering alone until dawn pinks the clouds.

☐ The FBI pursues a serial killer who targets criminals who have committed terrible offenses. Law enforcement struggles to follow the killer's trail; the public is sympathetic to the vigilante, a sentiment that is also shared by officers within the force

☐   An heirloom of incredible value is believed to be cursed, as its owners always die within a month of accepting the item for safe-keeping.

There is no curse, but one very determined and very distant family member who wants the heirloom for their own.

☐   Unaccompanied children begin to appear at a local bus stop. The police takes notice and brings the children in, hoping to find their parents. The children lack identification. They insist that they don't remember where they had been or how they had come to that specific bus stop.

☐   A family is stranded in a small, tourist town at the very end of the tourism season. Snow has fallen too deep to travel. The family extends their stay at the local inn; they find their hosts reluctant to accommodate them, and much less pleasant than they had been the rest of the vacation. In fact, the whole town seems eager to see the family go.

PARANORMAL

Tales of paranormal events capture the imagination. Indulge the reader and your own love of the supernatural with prompts that are anything but "normal."

☐ Falling in love with a dead man isn't all that great.

It's not that bad, either. Sure, the guy can't take you to the movies, but he's a *great* listener.

☐ A demon falls in love with a human. The human doesn't have the power to see creatures of the demon's ilk, and never will. Even so, the demon is incapable of letting go. It watches over its beloved human, helping out whenever the human is in need.

Write the tale from two points of view - that of the pining demon, and that of the human. Give the human a dangerous profession, where the demon's well-meant meddling is often the difference between life and death.

☐ A spirit and a human fight over an apartment. The spirit isn't leaving. Neither is the human - the rent's low, and the place's two blocks from work! The human would take a haunted apartment over rush-hour commute, anytime.

☐ Sasha is convinced that the new girl in his class is the heroine from a book he loves to death. He is half-right; the girl is indeed the heroine from Sasha's beloved story. In fact, it's Sasha's adoration that brought the girl to life.

Or rather, brought *something* to life. Fictional characters have little depth, and demons know how to use a loophole (and a love-struck fool) when they find one.

☐ Write a paranormal haunting story from the point of view of the ghost. Make the story creepy, threadbare, and half-insane - as a creature who ought to be long dead would experience the world.

☐ A girl picks up a lost pen. The pen is possessed. The girl's biology notes turn out strange indeed.

☐   Seeing a long-dead relative is bizarre enough. Having that relative demand you go visit their old, dilapidated house in search of a letter to deliver to an old lover is a whole new level of weird.

☐   A creature that eats nightmares falls in love with a man/woman whose nightly terrors feed it very, very well. The creature takes the shape of a human and approaches their beloved.

☐   A haunted house tries to get people to come inside. The house's just really lonely, and not all that bad - except the part where it won't let guests leave, never ever.

☐   Katryn takes in a street cat after finding the poor creature hurt behind a dumpster. She nurses the cat back to health.

The cat is in fact an agent from a top-secret government organization. He has suffered a momentary transfiguration after accidentally ingesting a drug the government has been tracking.

☐   Receiving messages from the beyond can be downright terrifying. Except for Clara, who is being haunted by the universe's most uptight spirit. She finds, "Put coasters under your drinks," scribbled on a post-it note one morning. In blood, but still.

☐   The ghost ships come every three years. People light lanterns and leave them along the shore, to mark land from water so no spirit wanders on dry earth by mistake. Nobody thinks of ensuring no mortal finds their way in the water come midnight. All who live by the sea know the legend and have seen the ships first-hand. Surely, no one would be foolish enough to board one of them...

☐   The Three Kings of Darkness are resurrected every five hundred years. Each time, they must seek their lighter halves in the mortal realm in order to come into their full power. Each King possesses a character flaw that is complimented by a strength found in their lighter half. The Kings scorn humanity, their hearts only ever kind to their fated companions.

☐ Sim used to be a Siamese cat. A witch, a wish, and some magic later, Sim is a person trying to navigate the bizarreness of life as a human as she/he seeks out her/his old owner, who had disappeared without a trace a month earlier.

☐ Finding the key to Hell's gates isn't half as exciting as it sounds. Kristin is dragged through a hellish (heh) bureaucratic process when she tries to return the darn thing, whisked from one Underworld aide's cubicle to another. A procession of paperwork and interrogations by scary-looking demons later, she is finally admitted to the Gatekeeper's office and gets her biggest shock yet: she knows the man sitting behind the desk. Or she thought she did, seeing as her boyfriend had never mentioned he was employed by freaking *hell*.

☐ A woman finds a way into the Underworld/ Heaven/the Afterlife in order to find her husband - and yell at him for daring to die before her. The spirits of the afterlife are bewildered, to say the least.

☐ Ghosts make for the best ghost-hunters.

☐ An overworked woman finds a stray kitten on her way home one night. It's raining, and the kitten looks downright pitiful huddling under the staircase leading up to the woman's lonely apartment. The woman takes the kitten home. She is too tired to notice much other than the animal being wet. For example, she completely misses the fact that its eyes are red, or that it has two tails rather than one.

☐ A demon with a phobia of humans accidentally stumbles into a magical circle, which traps the creature in a public elementary school. The demon is able to assume human guise for a period of time, but can't do anything about its fear of the tiny humans populating the school.

It gets even worse; one of the puny things decides to befriend the demon. The kid is hellishly persistent.

☐ A girl grows up talking to the strange creature buried in her grandparents' garden. No one else seems to realize the creature is there. The girl doesn't understand how people keep missing it - its head sticks out from the ground and everything!

☐ A man falls in love with a spirit. He decides to take his own life, in order to be with his beloved. The spirit is not willing to let the man die.

☐   Josh's band is making it big on the indie scene. They manage to land a gig opening for an established band in New York City. Josh is over the moon about it.

Too bad this is the time his estranged father decides to seek him out and indoctrinate him in the ways of vampires. Because Josh is half-vampire now, apparently.

It's all superb.

☐   Write about a realistic date between a human and a supernatural creature. Is it really romantic to share a meal with a furry werewolf? Or a blood-thirsty vampire? What kind of problems and/or hilarious situations arise?

☐   A haunted pen is sold to a writer. The pen has a mind of its own, writing whatever it pleases. Its new owner is bemused, but not afraid. He wishes to find out who the pen belonged to, and how it became animate.

☐   Phrase prompt: "Demon parade."

☐   A cursed hat ends up in a Salvation Army store. It is purchased by a teen girl putting together a Halloween costume. The girl is planning to dress up as a witch. On the night of the party, her assumed persona turns a little more real than she would have wished.

☐ The not-quite-departed soul of a woman's grandmother stands guard in the woman's home, vetting boyfriends and helping out with chores. The woman can't see her ghostly roommate, but ends up appreciating the otherworldly help.

☐ Every human dwelling has a house spirit to protect those who live within. If something bad happens to the home's owners, the spirit may retain the malicious energy and turn into a monster, preying on those it had once guarded.

☐ A high school class takes an overnight trip to a famous landmark. The bus runs over something while passing through a forest. The driver stops and goes to investigate - only to be mauled to death by what the class takes to be a wild animal. The teacher is able to start the bus up, but it's a slow going. There is nothing in pursuit of the bus, but it still doesn't seem like a good idea to stop and spend the night in the forest.

Thankfully, the group comes across a secluded hotel just before sundown.

☐ A vengeful spirit enters the body of a stray animal that is near death. The two spirits merge into a single being, and live on as a creature that is half-human, half-animal.

☐ A house built on the site of a long-ago battle is inhabited by two vengeful spirits - the generals leading the two opposing armies who had fought on that land so long ago. When a young family moves into the house, the generals find common ground in protecting the family's children from the other nasty spirits that have spawned on the property.

☐ Dogs are loyal to the end - and beyond. A young boy loses his dog. Years later, the boy - now a young man - is saved by a ghostly version of his old companion.

☐ Possession by a demon is an established cliché in the paranormal horror genre. Flip it on its head by having a demon seek a human host for an honorable reason, with the villains of the story being the humans the demon hunts.

☐ A woman discovers the power to summon ghosts. She uses that power to keep loneliness at bay, and ends up having more dead friends than living ones.

☐ A possessed toy finds lonely children and keeps them company, until they no longer have a need for it.

☐ A woman keeps running into people she knows - or rather, people she *knew*, when they were still alive.

☐ A woman has the gift of foresight. She has long ago given up on trying to change the future she sees, knowing that certain things are set in their paths. It is better to let Fate work her wheel.

When she sees someone dear to her come to harm, that particular piece of wisdom goes out the window. The woman must figure out how to alter what is to come, without contributing to the future she has foreseen.

☐ Not all ghosts are malicious, and not all who are haunted deserve to be saved.

☐ A paranormal detective stumbles onto a crime scene while pursuing a supernatural creature. The crime is in progress, and committed by humans. The creature the detective had been following decides to help the victims. The detective finds himself siding with the creature.

☐ A young child abandoned by his parents in the depths of a dark forest finds companionship with ghouls, goblins, and all kinds of scary creatures.

☐ A freak accident electrocutes a man. The electrical charge is great enough that it should have turned him to ash; instead, the man is phased out of reality by a nanosecond. This means he is able to see everyone and everything around him, but no one else can see him.

☐ The earrings the new Mrs. Miller is wearing are to die-for - literally. A vengeful spirit bleeds through the gold into the woman wearing them, poisoning the blood of its killer.

☐ A man dies. His spirit lingers on earth; at first, he is a solid, rational presence. As time passes, his grip on the human realm grows more precarious. He begins to lose his humanity and grows more malignant. In moments of clarity, the man searches for a way to find rest, not wishing to do anyone any harm.

☐ The ghost of a beloved TV personality haunts their old studio, appearing in various sitcoms and TV shows filmed there. Most of the actors working at the studio have come to terms with the ghostly intruder.

☐ Cats are envoys of the Underworld. They guide the spirits of the departed to their final rest. So if you see a cat walking with purpose in the dead of night, don't follow - there is already someone trailing in its paw-steps.

☐ A man receives a tarot card deck as a joke-present from a colleague. He deals a hand and reads it, using the guide that comes with the deck. According to the cards, the man has something dangerous dogging his every step.

☐ A man dies in a terribly embarrassing way. His spirit is unwilling to depart after meeting such a meaningless end. It sticks around, helping out people in trouble.

☐ Jay buys a motorcycle possessed by the spirit of a vigilante. The bike takes Jay superhero-ing, without any input on Jay's part.

☐ A masterful watchmaker dies while working on his latest creation. The clock remains unfinished; it charms buyer after buyer nonetheless, to their peril.

☐ Living on the same land of generations means living alongside the ghosts of a great many dead relatives. Most of them don't really care about the living.

Then there are those who won't stop butting into Kathy's business.

☐ Two spirits haunting neighboring houses fall in love. Each spirit is bound to its given property, and cannot cross into the other's territory. They resort to using the living as go-betweens.

☐ One night, a light flickers on in a rundown house. Ghostly faces begin to appear in the house's windows, accompanied by strange noises and blood-curling screams. News cameras soon flock the scene, but no one is brave enough to enter the property.

A reality TV star decides to capitalize on the house's popularity and use the space as the setting of their latest episode.

POETRY

to write a poem is
to paint the whole world with
but one drop of ink

☐ Write a poem about winter without using any words to do with snow or cold.

☐ Write a poem with attention to the sounds its words make when read aloud. Weave a melody within the text.

☐ Make note of three objects in your immediate vicinity. Include them in a poem; the sillier, the better!

☐ Write an insulting poem. Whether you take on the persona of a bard making fun of nobility, or channel some of your real-world frustrations, make sure your piece is both mocking and hilarious.

☐   What does the month of February mean to you? Do you associate it with love (Valentine's Day), empowerment (Black History Month in the US; LGBT History Month in the UK), or something personal? Write a poem around the month and its meaning to you. Free-verse.

☐   Write a companion-piece to a famous poem. It can be a continuation of the poem, a prequel, a different POV, a mirror theme - whatever you like, as long as the reference to the original is there.

Poems you could consider:

- *The Road not Taken*, Robert Frost
- *The Raven*, Edgar Allan Poe
- *may i feel said he*, E. E. Cummings

☐   Write a sonnet. Points for an unusual subject; that is, in a genre beside romance and tragedy.

☐   Write a happy poem featuring an animal. Make it something a child would like to read.

☐   Experiment with a short poem in a style you have never composed in before.

☐ Write an epic-style poem to commemorate a small, silly personal victory. Slaying cockroaches, learning how to ride a bike, sneaking home way after curfew - anything goes. The sillier, the better. Remember to exalt your deeds at great length. Throwing out the names of a few Greek gods would also not go amiss. Did Ares guide your hand as it squashed that mosquito mid-air? You bet'cha.

☐ Write a poem about sleep. Make the reader feel like they want to take a nap after reading.

☐ Write a war-poem. The inspiration can be ancient, half-fantastical battle of the kind depicted by the *Aeneid* or the *Iliad*, or a modern, tech-heavy struggle.

☐ Write a lover's poem. Make it passionate, focusing on beat and imagery.

☐ How would a poem written by a robot - not an AI, just a robot programmed to match tempo/ rhyme/etc. - read? Do your best robo-imitation.

☐ A cat has written you a poem. What does it say?

☐ Write a poem that references celestial bodies.

☐ Write a poem that symbolizes hope. Take care to keep the poem feeling light and joyful to read.

☐ Write a haiku that contains the following three words, one per line if you can manage it: spring/wine/song.

☐ Write a poem you would love to receive as a gift from someone else.

☐ In a number of ancient societies, poetry and letter writing of all kinds was nobility's preferred way of communication.

Write three letters, each one including a poem as part of the text. The first letter is shared between friends, the second between lovers, and the third - between enemies.

☐ There's nothing worse than a poet in love.

Write a story interwoven with poems, written by a love-struck teen to his possibly-would-be-girlfriend. If she's able to withstand all the mushy missives that find their way into her locker, that is.

☐ Write a poem written by the Grim Reaper.
Dark humor challenge.

☐   Compose a poem about growing up. Each stanza should be its own "period of life," however you would like to define the term.

☐   Write a poem that would make the reader blush, in a good way.

☐   Write a poem dedicated to your favorite literary character.

☐   Two crows sit on a telephone line in winter. They croak to each other as humans trudge by, heads bent against the falling snow. Write their conversation as a poem.

☐   Even beloved people can be a pain in the behind. Write a poem that sweetly chastises someone over a rude habit.

☐   Write a tale styled as a poem, with a young audience in mind. Feature at least two woodland animals.

☐   Write a pumpkin-flavored poem.

☐   Write a poem in which each stanza begins with the words, 'I am.'

☐ Write a lullaby poem - stanzas meant to soothe the reader.

☐ Write a poem meant for younger readers. Make it happy and playful.

☐ Write a simple poem (in a form of your choosing) that can be used as a tool to teach beginners about poetry, meter, and rhythm. Write a short description of the poem, educating readers about its structure.

☐ A fox turns into a human and goes to play in a human village. Write a poem around the fox's game.

☐ Capture the concept of transience in a poem.

☐ Many news outlets have a photography section, where beautiful photographs of nature, history, and daily life are featured. Choose one such photo and write a poem about its subject.

☐ Summer has dyed to autumn gold and red. Write a poem about the changing seasons, with attention to color and physical sensations.

☐ Write a poem that spans a single day, beginning with sunrise and ending with sunset.

☐ Compose a poem that can double as an advertisement for a specific product from a well-known brand.

☐ Experiment with poetic structure. Try to create your own type of poem, be it in shape or in meter.

☐ Write an angry poem.

☐ Compose a poem featuring a transformation, whether of nature or a transfiguration of a human soul.

☐ Write a poem using only emoji.

☐ Capture the feeling of a relaxing day on the beach in a poem. Focus on mood.

☐ Write a poem inspired by your favorite song. The poem should do one of the following: 1) match the song in rhythm; 2) have the same theme/message as the song; 3) include words from the song's lyrics, in a manner that clearly calls back to the original text.

☐ Erato, the Greek Muse of lyric poetry, speaks to you in your dreams. Write the poem she whispers in your ear.

☐ Write a fun, quirky poem meant for children, encouraging kids to eat their fruits and veggies.

☐ Dedicate a poem to someone important in your life. Style the poem so it matches their personality, wording the poem to fit this person's manner of speech and character.

☐ Dissect one of your favorite poems, making note of: 1) tempo; 2) style; 3) theme/imagery. Write a "sequel" poem that matches the original in all three aspects.

☐ Write a poem that is exactly 13 lines long, and includes as many unlucky omens as possible.

☐ Wait until you are sleepy - either late at night, or in the early morning. Write a poem without planning or thinking, noting words down as they come to mind.

☐ Come up with a funny, memorable limerick.

# **R** EALISM

Depict the world as it truly is, grounding your reader in reality and the present. Fact really is stranger than fiction, and worthy of a tale or two - or exactly 52, as many as the prompts in this section!

☐ Write a story in which the characters change, but the setting remains the same. Focus the story on a small geographic location; for example, a single room in a house/apartment or a bench in a public park. Time can be as fluid as you like.

☐ A college student under a ton of pressure takes a break from work, studies, and relationships to enjoy a cup of coffee. Write the scene, focusing on the student's internal state. Start from a point of chaos, with the character growing more peaceful by degrees.

☐ Choose a craft - painting, woodworking, knitting... Something physical. Create a story around a character working on a project in that craft. Focus on their vision as a creator, but don't forget to give the reader snippets of their increasingly messy environment, the character's physical state, and all else that would make your audience feel as if they are the ones shaping something into being.

☐ A person is hiking through a deep forest, alone. They are familiar with their surroundings. Write the story in 3rd POV, emphasizing the person's interaction with their environment. Convey their peace and happiness in being by themselves. Try not to use any dialogue.

☐ Two characters go about their day. One is an investor banker. The other is a janitor at an international airport. Tell the story from both perspectives, running in parallel to each other.

☐ Write a "slice of life" story, featuring a single scene from an ordinary day of a couple cohabitating in a busy metropolitan city. Create a mood of comfort around their home.

☐ Write a story of an everyday encounter between two people. Structure the tale so the readers follow both characters in parallel tales as they go about their day, culminating with their meeting.

☐ Write a short scene featuring a student trying not to fall asleep during lecture. They've been up the previous night and are absolutely dying for sleep, but their 9am professor takes attendance and so, there they are.

Have the reader stifling yawns as they sympathize with the student's pained need for sleep.

☐ Write of a man/woman who has lived an entirely normal, perfectly boring life. Set up the tedium of their workplace and home in the beginning of the story. Introduce a twist in a most unusual, exciting event happening to a character who has known only dullness. Do they witness a crime? Severely hurt someone by accident? Bump into a celebrity? Get tailed by an undercover FBI agent in a case of mistaken identity? Anything is possible, as long as it remains in the realm of the "real."

☐ Center a tale about a family that has recently emigrated to a foreign country. Balance their struggles with the good things about living in this new place, from culture to people to new opportunities.

☐ A character of advanced age lives alone in a lovely, but lonely, cottage in England. Follow the character during a normal day in their life. Have their joys and quiet sorrows shine through actions, showing rather than telling.

☐ A girl finds an expensive camera. She goes through the recorded photos, trying to find out the identity of the camera's owner. In the process, she builds a story in her head of the person's life based on the pictures they have taken.

☐ Two old women sit on a bench in front of a house and gossip. People pass by. A stray cat sits at the women's feet, mewing for attention.

Write the scene in true realist style - no romanticizing of action or overly ornate language. Make the story direct and poignant.

☐   A woman starts a second life in her mid-fifties. She is far happier than she ever was before, even in her youth and the height of love. Describe her new life and what makes her so content.

☐   Tell a story about a kitchen in a university-owned housing unit/dormitory from two POVs: One belonging to a student who lives at this particular house, and another of a member of the cleaning staff assigned to care for the house. The story can be explicitly about the kitchen, or simply take place within the kitchen area.

☐   Write about someone who is not a realist, in that they pursue their dreams despite limitations imposed by money, time, or geographic location. Set the story at the moment this character achieves their ultimate goal. Have them think about the sacrifices and struggles that had led them to their present victory. The challenge: Make the story and the character's journey realistic, with their extraordinary accomplishment fitting logically into the grand plan of their life.

☐   An adult discovers a box of childhood memorabilia in their closet. They go through the box, and the memories that go along with the items inside.

☐ Write a short scene from the perspective of a graduate student attempting to balance their studies and job during the week of final exams. Insert a romantic drama into the mix for full-on chaos.

☐ Create a story in which everything is logical, orderly, and true to the real world except one single component. That could be a character, a place, or even an object.

☐ A person sits in a cafe, working on their laptop. Describe the scene. Include descriptions of the cafe interior, the staff, and other patrons, creating a patchwork of human interactions around the stationary figure of the patron.

☐ Tell the story of a young person going to their first job interview. Include their preparation for the interview, the interview itself, and the aftermath - the period of waiting to hear back, culminating with that most-important phone call. Focus on emotion; invest the reader in the character's fate.

☐ Write about a teen party from the point of view of someone who really, really doesn't like parties. They were dragged there by a friend - who has conveniently disappeared since arriving - and must now brave the event on their own.

☐ A couple goes hiking for the very first time. They get lost, eat some questionable berries, meet a bear, almost start a forest fire... Long story short, they're never going hiking again.

☐ Capture the feeling of displacement that comes with moving somewhere new - be it a new city, a new country, or even simply a new house. Tailor the emotions to the specific character's personality. Some may find more wonder and joy in being in a new place; others may feel apprehensive, or even fearful.

☐ The circus is in town! The fortune-teller is particularly busy, with people of all ages and backgrounds dropping in to catch a glimpse of their future. Tell of several sessions from the point of view of the Diviner him/herself, keeping in mind that he/she is an actor and cannot tell fortune to save his/her life.

☐ Walk a mile in someone else's shoes! Write a story about an argument you had with someone, but tell it from the other person's perspective. You may think you were right - but then again, so did they.

☐ Tell a story from the perspective of a songbird that was captured from the wild, and now lives in a birdcage. Do not humanize the bird, but do describe its perception of its changed environment and the loss of its home.

☐ A hiker encounters a wild animal on their way up a dangerous trail. The animal itself doesn't pose an immediate threat, but could do so if provoked. The hiker can't pass without alerting the animal to their presence.

Describe the encounter, with focus on the animal and its reactions.

☐ Two friends are out for coffee. They have known each other for years, but are not close in the way true friends are. Write a story centered around their conversation, which tends toward the trite and shallow.

☐ Write a story focused on a single family and their experience of Halloween - from decorating, to creating costumes, to trick-or-treating and the inevitable sugar high.

☐ Realists are not necessarily pessimists. Write a story in which being grounded in reality is a good thing, with the main protagonist observing others living in made-up, shallow worlds.

☐   A serious, slightly gloomy child befriends a classmate who is their total opposite in terms of personality. Describe a scene of the two children at play.

☐   Describe a session at the gym. If possible, draw on your own experiences and set the tale in a specific establishment. Is everyone necessarily there to work out? Any regulars? Underline the strangeness of a seemingly ordinary space.

☐   The son of a small-town baker quits his high-paying job in the city to come home and take over the family business. The whole town is trying to figure out the reason, but the man is not easy to talk to and his family won't say a word about any of it. The local gossip mill is busy working up stories, but all fall far from the truth.

☐   Growing up means letting go of some things, whether due to having grown out of them or because it is the socially acceptable course of action. Write a story in which a character gives up something they had held dear during childhood, whether a friend or a hobby or even an aspect of their own personality.

☐ A single father is juggling work, house chores, and taking care of his child, all the while fighting off well-meaning but utterly annoying comments by his friends and neighbors urging him to find a new partner.

☐ Re-imagine your life by changing a single, key aspect of your current identity - be it your gender, religion, or the nation in which you were born. What would your life be like, in this alternate universe? What would stay the same?

☐ An artist suffering from a severe creativity slump leaves his studio to wander around town, hoping to find inspiration. What does he see? Who/what does he paint upon returning home?

☐ A man sits at the banks of a river. A woman passes by on the road above. The two do not know each other, and never will - theirs is one among hundreds of missed connections that happen every day.

☐ Set a spooky scene in a real place that you know well. Describe the sound of trees rustling at twilight, shadows stretching over familiar grounds, wind chimes clinking along windows...

☐ Life is a series of choices - a maze of diverging paths that we travel blindly. Tell a story in which several characters struggle with indecision in a situation where the "right" choice is not readily apparent. The conundrums the characters face should range from mild to severe, with their stories either weaving together or running parallel to each other, delivering a single overall message to the reader.

☐ A woman marries a man and becomes a step-mother to his two children. Write of her struggle to fit into this existing family.

☐ Kids can't wait to grow up. Adults wish to be kids again.

Write about a group of adults acting like children, having the time of their lives.

☐ A man has moved to a large city for work. Everything is unfamiliar, the man's friends and family are far away, and the job proves more challenging and stressful than the man had expected. How does the man approach his situation? What is his outlook on life? Ground the story in the man's specific personality, leaving a clear image of him as a person in the reader's mind.

☐ A man struggling with personal problems shakes off his gloom and rediscovers the beauty of the world while on an ordinary stroll through town.

☐ A child and an adult in their early thirties talk about what they want to be when they grow up. The child is full of enthusiasm and ideas. The adult, jaded from their experience in the workforce, finds some inspiration and hope by listening to the child's dreams of the future.

☐ Last-minute gift-shopping means crowded malls, trips through heavy snow, and fighting for the last item on the shelf. Capture the madness in a story. Make your character a Grinch who has been forced to host a holiday party, but nonetheless finds themselves unwilling to disappoint their family.

☐ Jane Murray's family is made up of people with strong characters and unique views on life. There is not a single boring day in their household. Guests, on the other hand, find the experience of life with the Murrays quite...interesting.

☐ Jessica gets in trouble with her parents. She has her cell confiscated as punishment, and must face a whole week in high school without a phone.

☐ Paul pursues his dreams of being a famous artist. Each year is harder than the next, and he soon finds himself struggling to make ends meet. He can't give up, latching onto every glimmer of hope life throws his way.

☐ A capricious, childish person discovers that the world doesn't revolve around them and their wants the hard way. They must now rebuild their life and relationship with those they have hurt in their ignorant days.

☐ Anita is a NEET - a young person who is "Not in Education, Employment, or Training." On top of that, she is a shut-in; she lives with her parents and largely keeps to her own room, fearful of the outside world and all of its complications.

A past classmate of Anita's hears of her troubles, and decides to visit. The two click in a way they never had in school, and find something special in a world both perceive as difficult in different ways.

ROMANCE

Love gives us hope, makes life worth living, and serves as a crucial ingredient in any story hoping to attract an audience's affection. The prompts that follow are both bitter and sweet, as befitting of this most emotional genre. Put your rose-tinted glasses on, and grab a pen!

☐   Write a story of romance gone wrong. Start with the break-up and go backwards, ending with the very first, "I love you" the couple shares.

☐   Tell a story about someone who doesn't want to be in love. The complexities that come with loving someone - the compromises, the vulnerability, the co-dependence - aren't this person's cup of tea. They certainly aren't looking for their soulmate.

They don't have to look; Ms./Mr. Perfect finds *them.*

☐ Write about a couple sitting together in a cafe from an outsider's POV. The narrator can't hear what the couple is saying to each other. Their love is apparent from their gestures.

☐ Write about an unusual romance between two unlikely people. The relationship shouldn't be a taboo, but rather simply unlikely. Say, the crown princess of a small European country dating a barista. Or a seemingly bitter, sarcastic person having the sweetest significant other. In all cases, the couples must be head over heels in love.

☐ A boy gives his crush home-made chocolates for St. Valentine's Day. Cue food-poisoning, a trip to the school nurse, and falling in love over botched chocolate treats.

☐ An overprotective parent meets their child's significant other for the first time. The girl/boyfriend is perfect. The parent tries to find a fault in them, fails, but keeps being suspicious anyway.

Recommended cross-genre: Humor.

☐   A woman falls in love with a singer after listening to his songs. She goes to concerts, buys his CDs, and loves him more and more with every beautiful song she hears.

What the woman doesn't know is that the singer doesn't write his own songs. The real artist - the person she has actually fallen in love with - is much closer to home than she realizes.

☐   Write a fairy-tale like meeting set in the modern world. There is instant connection between the characters, a spark of attraction that runs deeper than the physical - a shared moment in time.

☐   Role reversal challenge! Have a woman play "prince charming" for her sweetheart, a "lad in distress."

☐   Build a romance through interaction. Have your characters fall in love after spending time together, getting used to each other's rough edges and slowly allowing themselves to be who they are beyond the usual, polite personas they display to the world.

☐   A witch summons what she believes to be a demon, and sends him to plague a female warrior who has continuously ruined the witch's plans. Only the creature is no demon, but rather a confused man from modern times sucked into an alternative universe by the witch's spell. The man goes to do the witch's bidding, fearing being discovered for a fraud and hoping he would be able to run away while the witch is not looking. Unfortunately, the witch has means of monitoring the man's movements and the ability to recall him back to her side at moment's notice.

☐   Write a story about a perfect relationship. Perfection doesn't mean clichéd romance - although it could include some of that! - but two very real people loving each other despite their flaws and the stress of the world around them.

Try to portray this perfect love in a single scene. Be it the couple watching TV, basking in sunlight on the beach, or discussing something inconsequential. Ensure the love shines through, and that the relationship is healthy and happy.

☐   The bad boy falls in love with the top student in his class. Only class president is hiding a pretty dark side of her own, and is way more badass than her delinquent admirer. In the end, who did the boy fall in love with? The persona, or the real girl beneath?

☐   They don't fit. They never have, and never will, and all the love in the world won't make it so they can be together. They care for each other from afar instead, taking whatever joy they can from making the other happy.

This is a Romeo and Juliet story without the passionate romance and the unhappy ending. The protagonists do not end up together, but are overall happy with their lives.

☐   Maki falls in love with a fictional character. She is obsessed enough to have a literal shrine of merchandise of her imagined beau in her room.

An exchange student bearing incredible likeliness to Maki's beloved character joins the girl's class. Maki may just fangirl herself to death - or at the very least, into a major case of embarrassment.

☐ Rivalry turns into obsession, then a not-so-friendly romance. Write a story about a power-couple no one ever wants to hang out with on account of all the shouting and arguing and unintentionally mushy love-scenes.

☐ A person travels back thousands of years, to an ancient civilization of which no trace survives today. The person is stuck in this time period for a number of years. Initially bereft and homesick, she/he finds unexpected companionship - and love. Love like she/he has never experienced before.

The person travels back to their own time, whether by choice or happenstance. They miss the loved one they'd left behind terribly. Imagine their surprise upon finding a familiar face on an outing in the city. Turns out, reincarnation is very real - as is the concept of soulmates.

☐ Falling in love with someone online - a person you've never met or spoken to, other than through pixels - is not exactly ideal. Especially when your online crush turns out to be a music idol with whom you've been in star-struck love for years.

☐   A girl is in love with her dorky best friend. Now, if she could only get her feelings through to him somehow - you know, without actually having to say anything.

☐   A couple who has broken up finds the most ridiculous excuses to meet up, usually by dragging their friends along to places where they can "accidentally" bump into their ex. Said friends are not amused.

☐   Write about a budding romance from the point of view of a bystander; for example, a close friend or a sibling. Have the bystander meddle from time to time. The couple-to-be is playing coy, unsure of the other's feelings. Your MC has had just about enough of them pining after each other, and prods them along.

☐   Unrequited love challenge: Your character is in love with their best friend. That friend is going through a tough breakup. Your character is trying their best to support them without showing their true feelings.

☐   Everyone thinks Julie and Sam are dating. That's news to Julie and Sam, who certainly like each other, but haven't had the guts to confess yet.

☐ Anne is in love with someone who is beyond kind to her, and terribly cruel to others. She tries to justify her love for this person to herself, but cannot. What does she do, in the end?

☐ A man with a kind heart but intimidating face has trouble finding friends, let alone love. Until he meets a person who is his exact opposite - a sweet face covering a really short temper. They fall together like pieces of a puzzle.

☐ Karl has a habit of falling for the most unsuitable girls. He enlists his friends' help in navigating the dating business. Said friends didn't realize how hard a job they were signing up for.

☐ While cleaning out her apartment, a woman discovers a framed bouquet of pressed flowers. The flowers had been a gift from a past love. The woman thinks about who she used to be and what could have been.

☐ Two friends pretend to be in love in order to get out of bad dates set up by their matchmaking families. The "pretend" part of the equation doesn't last past their own first pretend-date.

☐   A man tries to do something romantic for his girlfriend in an attempt to earn her forgiveness. His understanding of what constitutes "romantic" could use some work.

☐   Two people keep on running into each other, ending up in situations where one would help the other out with something small - be it by ceding a taxi, loaning an umbrella, or giving directions to an unknown part of town. They come to like each other, but are never able to talk long enough to make plans for a more casual meeting.

Until they realize that they had been living across the street from each other all along.

☐   A master criminal cooks up an amazing heist to impress his equally deviant girlfriend.

☐   An AI falls in love with a human, in a world where AI and humans coexist.

Tell a story of the AI attempting to court their chosen human, from the AI's perspective. While AI are capable of emotion similar to those experienced by humans, they still process stimuli and "think" as machines - in logical, practical steps. Ensure the voice of the story matches the POV.

☐   A sudden storm traps several people in the lobby of their company building. Most of those assembled are strangers to each other, as they work for different branches of the company and thus rarely cross paths.

Unbeknownst to all, the company's CEO - a man who makes no public appearances, allowing the head of the Board of Executives to take his place in the spotlight - is also weathering the storm in the lobby. He studies his employees, gauging their overall satisfaction with their work and listening for any warning signs of internal dysfunction. A scathing conversation between a new employee and her well-established, but lazy coworker catches his attention.

☐   A young woman is determined to find love, but keeps meeting the wrong men. When Mr. Right finally comes along, she might be too jaded to recognize him.

Thankfully, Fate and her one true love do not give up easily.

☐   A couple is cursed with the worst luck on their dates. Humorous disasters dog their every outing, but can't detract from their happiness at simply being with each other.

☐   Two people have been living together and taking care of each other for over ten years. They are neither married nor romantically involved.

☐   Hana and Steve are constantly mistaken for a couple. They are really just close friends. Unfortunately, they are so close that any potential date thinks the two in love.

☐   A woman agrees to a date set up by her mother and a professional match-maker. The date ends up a bust, and the woman meets the man of her dreams - only it isn't her date partner.

☐   Two characters keep crossing paths in a shared space of some sort - a dormitory kitchen, a Laundromat, the cafeteria at work, etc. They slowly start to like each other.

     Write this budding romance as it develops, through ten meetings in a shared space of your choice.

☐   Vicky runs an animal shelter. One day, a man brings a dog he'd found by the side of the road to her door. He ends up coming by quite often, supposedly to check up on the dog and in spite of a severe allergy to canines.

☐ One ordinary day, a man receives a large bouquet of roses at work. His coworkers are bewildered. The man himself thinks the delivery is some sort of mistake, but finds the attached card very much addressed to him.

Despite his outward embarrassment, the man finds being on the receiving end of courting gifts surprisingly pleasant.

☐ An office worker moonlights as a famous romance author. She writes her current crush - a colleague at her day job - as the lead in her latest novel. When she sees a copy of the book on said colleague's desk, she panics and asks him about it. The man turns out to be a huge fan of her writer persona. He confesses to have fallen in love with the female heroine in this last book - who is modeled after the woman's own character.

☐ On a miserable day filled with mishaps, a woman is trudging home with an almost visible cloud of gloom over her head. She passes by a store that has recently opened. The mascot in front of the store - a giant bunny - hands her a heart-shaped balloon. The woman smiles for the first time that day.

Make this chance meeting the beginning of an adorable love story.

☐ Write a story featuring a kiss, with the kiss itself being the focus.

☐ A woman knits a sweater for her boyfriend. Said boyfriend gives the sweater to his roommate, who treasures the gift much more.

☐ A dating site suffers a system error, leading to several hundred members being matched to unsuitable partners. One such match ends up fortunate instead of faulty.

☐ A high school holds a festival in order to raise money for extracurricular activities. Clubs participate by putting up stalls or attractions for visitors to attend. One club sets up a palm-reading booth. Members of the club take turns telling tall-tales of their visitors' future. The number one question of interest concerns finding true love. One of the club's members proves a touch clairvoyant - every match he/she foretells ends up being perfect.

☐ Jeremy pulls a particularly stupid stunt at school. His parents send him to live with his grandparents in the countryside, for a fresh perspective on life and a little distance from his troublemaking friends. Jeremy is quickly put to work helping on the family farm. He just as quickly messes up by losing his grandfather's favorite horse. Jeremy's search for the equine leads him to a neighboring farm and a girl bound to break his heart.

☐ A woman dining alone finds a diamond ring in her dessert. She speaks with the waiter and, having located the owner of the ring, waits until the man leaves the table before approaching him to return it. As it turns out, the mistake had been fortunate - the man has just been dumped by his long-term girlfriend, and has no need for the ring.

☐ Richard has long given up on the whole love business. He focuses on his career instead, pushing away loneliness with long hours at the office.

One day, the one meant for him comes knocking at Richard's door - quite literally.

☐ Carol is terrible at all things romance. Her new boyfriend is her complete opposite in this regard. She tries her best to match his enthusiasm, but fails at every turn. Ultimately, she realizes that she is loved for the way she is and worries no more.

☐ A police officer and a thief fall in love during a bank robbery. One of the two is in civilian garb during the heist - either the officer is not on duty, or the thief isn't taking part in the robbery but is simply at the bank by chance.

CIENCE FICTION

SciFi tells tales of the far-off future, spectacular technology, and alien visitors. Stories in this genre demand logic and innovation in equal measures. Glimpse future possibilities for all of mankind in the prompts below!

☐ Deena was born on Magellan XVI - an advanced spacecraft on a decade-long exploratory mission. Deena grows up in the company of adults in a contained, logical environment. When Magellan XVI returns to Earth, she finds herself unable to assimilate into Earth culture or connect with her peers.

Deena longs to return to space. She finds comfort in the one object she had been allowed to keep from her time aboard Magellan XVI: A rock from a small, uninhabited planet. When cracks appear in the rock's smooth surface, Deena realizes that space may not be that far away after all.

☐   Earth has established a beta colony on Mars. Crops are being planted and the terrain altered, with the goal of eventually hosting a civilian city on the planet.

Jane's boyfriend, Ran, is among the scientists working on the colony. They talk as often as time and technology allows. During one of their calls, Jane notices something strange in the video feed. There are flickers of motion behind Ran - shadows that seem almost corporal. Jane convinces herself they are due to problems with the connection.

The shadows are thicker during the next call. The following week, Ran doesn't call at all.

☐   A man turns back time in order to save someone dear to him. However, nothing in Fate's plan is without a purpose; the person the man saves goes on to reshape the world in a truly terrifying way. The man himself is stuck in a time-loop, which he cannot break without outside help.

☐   A tech genius creates AI. By mistake. All of the appliances in the tech's house are now sentient - and adorably protective of their human maker.

▢   A small, round object falls from the sky. Chyou is convinced it belongs to a god. Her parents humor her; her two siblings make fun of her carrying around junk as if it's a treasure. One night, Chyou accidentally drops the orb into her tea.

It speaks.

▢   Earth is not a planet. It's a spaceship covered in cosmic dust and vegetation over billions of years. The ship is functional, its shields still up, the engines rumbling every once in a while - the true cause of earthquakes. Only a descendant of its original crew can activate its machinery.

An immense earthquake swallows half a town. A person wakes up days after the quake many, many miles underground. They appear to be floating in midair. The ship's shield has caught them, cushioning their fall.

They are a descendant of the crew who had piloted the ship.

▢   Aliens monitor our planet, much like security guards do local malls. An alien assigned a two-year shift in Earth's orbit decides to beam up a cat for company.

The beaming machine has a *slight* malfunction, and the cat's human owner finds themselves somewhere far, far away from home.

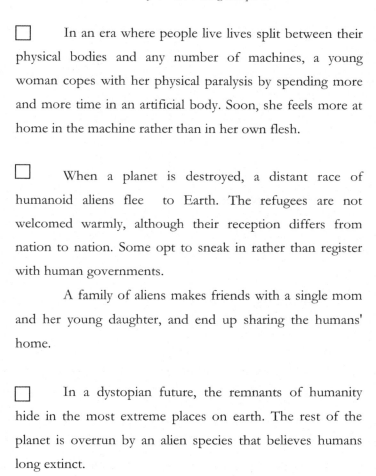

☐   In an era where people live lives split between their physical bodies and any number of machines, a young woman copes with her physical paralysis by spending more and more time in an artificial body. Soon, she feels more at home in the machine rather than in her own flesh.

☐   When a planet is destroyed, a distant race of humanoid aliens flee to Earth. The refugees are not welcomed warmly, although their reception differs from nation to nation. Some opt to sneak in rather than register with human governments.

A family of aliens makes friends with a single mom and her young daughter, and end up sharing the humans' home.

☐   In a dystopian future, the remnants of humanity hide in the most extreme places on earth. The rest of the planet is overrun by an alien species that believes humans long extinct.

One day, an alien youngling stumbles upon a human encampment and makes friends with a human family.

☐ The human race descends from an alien species that left Earth millions of years ago, deserting some of its population. Since, humanity has evolved to adapt to Earth's conditions. When our alien ancestors return, they find us much more different and difficult to deal with than they expect.

Suggested genre: humor. Try to fit in aliens struggling to understand modern pop-culture.

☐ A medical discovery rocks the world: Science is now able to treat ageing. The miracle serum does have a side effect, however - a fact the test group volunteers discover the hard way.

☐ Start your story with the following sentence:
"My best friend is an alien."

☐ A cosmic storm passes over Earth. It doesn't lead to natural disasters - it infects all living things it touches, boosting a random trait to extraordinary proportions. Some people gain superpowers.

Others become monsters.

☐   Humanity has discovered immortality - or rather, the science of harvesting souls. The process is relatively simple: Soulgems, rare crystals capable of hosting the energy of a person's soul, are fit to robotic frames after the degradation of a person's organic body. The soul within lives on indefinitely.

Soulgems sell for extraordinary amounts. As such, only the very rich can hope to secure immortality. Unless, of course, a mistake of some tragic sort occurs and the wrong soul is put in a waiting gem. Since the robotic body is created in the image of the person it was meant to host, and all involved in the procedure believe it to have been a success, no one is aware of the mix-up except the person who wakes up in a new body rather than - well, dead.

☐   An archeologist finds a strange object in a newly discovered tomb in Egypt. The object is buried with an unknown Pharaoh, and looks a whole lot like a cell phone. Laid in gold and covered in hieroglyphs, but still - very much a cell phone.

Stranger yet, the device turns on as soon as the archeologist touches it. It seems to be calling someone.

☐ In the near future, people have developed the technology to store memories as we now do photos. Virtual albums of memories are created and shared among family members. This means people are able to hold onto much more of their lives and remember their dear ones vividly, long after they are gone.

However, no tech is hack-proof. It is one thing to steal what people have recorded; when a malicious organization figures out how to hack into memories, the game changes entirely.

☐ Time as we know it is in the hands of creatures not of planet Earth. The clock is massive, and counts time in all directions and all ways.

One Friday the 13th, the clock malfunctions.

It seems a small glitch at first. The creatures responsible for the clock's upkeep scramble to find the cause. Meanwhile, on Earth, time threads are crossing over - past, present, and future interweave into a giant knot.

☐ A scientists travels 50 years into the future, testing a machine she has been secretly creating for most of her adult life. She selects the amount of time to travel carefully, believing that the world wouldn't have changed too much in the course of a few decades. After all, this is a trial run - she is not aiming for anything too ambitious beyond actually making it into the future.

The machine works, but the scientist's predictions are wrong. The world is almost unrecognizable, and not because it has turned into a post-apocalyptic wasteland. Rather the opposite, in fact. The scientist appears in a lush field, surrounded on all sides by beautiful natural sights. Blue skies, blooming flowers, air clean and crisp with spring - it is a joy simply existing in this wondrous place.

The only thing missing? Humans.

☐ Enhancer drugs exist. They are heavily regulated, and usually reserved for the use of individuals employed in tasking professions where a boost in mental or physical capabilities will be beneficial to society as a whole. The drugs can be taken only for brief periods of time, or will otherwise become toxic and inflict terrible side-effects.

A knock-off enhancer hits the black market. Its use is unregulated and its side-effects - devastating.

☐   A disaster on a distant planet brings a spaceship of alien refugees to Earth. The aliens in question are humanoid, but different enough that fitting into human society undetected would be impossible.

Choose the country in which the ship lands and the government's response. Does the country welcome the alien newcomers and announce them to the public? Do they imprison them, fearing no repercussions since the aliens' home planet no longer exists?

Meanwhile, the reason for the aliens' flight - an old enemy responsible for their planet's destruction - is making its way toward Earth.

☐   The discovery of a new element allows humanity to see something many would have much rather preferred hidden: The existence of a mirror realm populated by humanoid creatures who believe themselves to be the one and true species meant to rule Earth. They are unable to cross into our realm, but knowing the threat is there has everyone on edge - and some powerful people doing some very, very foolish things.

☐   A technician electrocutes himself while working on a top-line supercomputer. His body dies. His mind flees into the machine, connecting with the high-tech robotics within in ways no one could have predicted.

☐   A thousand years from now, society has been split into two classes. One lives in a utopia of shining cities and wealth.

The other is what remains of humanity.

☐   A girl builds a time portal from her grandmother's wonky old TV set - or rather, builds a machine that acts as a conduit and allows an older version of the girl to be pulled into this reality. That older version of the girl had built a portal in her own time, and tuned it in to this particular moment. There is something the girl must know, something important enough that her older self had bent time and space to reach her.

☐   Twin girls are playing together in their shared bedroom. One of the girls is an android - a replica of the sister the other girl had lost in early childhood. Neither is aware that anything is different between them.

☐ An alien has landed on Earth several thousand years ago. It lives in a swamp, in what used to be a wild, densely-forested area. The alien finds its territory shrinking as human cities expand. Finally, the swamp itself comes under threat.

The alien decides to take action and protect its home.

☐ There is a kingdom on the dark side of the moon, populated by people who are visually indistinguishable from humans. This society is in fact the origin of humanity as a species. They prefer to keep hidden from their Earthly brethren, but do keep tabs on what is happening on the Blue Planet. Some of the more adventurous Moon people even journey to Earth and interact with the creatures living there.

One such visit goes wrong in the worst way. Not only is the Moon person involved in grave danger, but extraction is nearly impossible without alerting Earthlings of alien presence. With no other options, the Moon kingdom contacts an ex-patriot who has made their home on Earth some decades prior, asking for their help.

☐ An alien delegation makes a number of hilarious cultural blunders during their first-contact expedition to the planet Earth.

☐　Things start to go missing in Miranda's home. They are small items, nothing worth stealing. More curiously, the objects tend to reappear after a few days. Miranda thinks her own mind is playing tricks on her. That is, until she finds the indentation of a small, three-fingered hand in her tube of ice cream.

There is something in Miranda's house alright, and it's not of this Earth.

☐　The old Barrett farmhouse has been the site of a number of strange, late-night sightings featuring bright lights and flying objects. Local folks avoid the area. UFO hunters camp within and around the house's ruins often, but can't seem to stay awake long enough to record anything of interest. Mechanical means of keeping watch - cameras and other technology - doesn't work properly on the Barrett's grounds.

One night, a child sneaks into the farm and disappears. A search party is organized by locals, headed by the police. A week later, there is still no sign of the lost kid.

A young man appears in the house two weeks later. He calls himself by the young child's name, and says he has been in another world entirely for the last twenty years - a place where time flows differently than on Earth.

☐ An alien spacecraft lands on Earth, thousands of years in the past. An ancient civilization witnesses the landing. Write a story from the perspective of a member of this civilization, and their perception of the strange events.

☐ A young man saves someone from danger. He is severely hurt in the process; the pain the injury causes pales in comparison to the shock he experiences when he sees the wound close on its own, knitting together to cover exposed cables and wiring where there should be blood and muscle.

☐ Decades into the future, humans make contact with an alien ship for the very first time. The aliens have suffered great damage to their vessel, and request permission to land on Earth. The government they contact grants it, with much enthusiasm from its scientific community.

The aliens in question are not aliens - they are a human crew that had lost its way during an exploratory mission. Time in space has altered their DNA and outward appearance, as well as their mental states. In the end, the crew that comes back to Earth is indeed closer to alien than human. They have a reason for concealing their true identity.

☐ An apocalypse turns back the clock on planet Earth. The few human survivors are exclusively children, and grow up without memory of their destroyed world. What kind of society do they create? How do they perceive the remnants of the past that have survived the disaster?

☐ An alien spacecraft needs to make an emergency landing on Earth. The craft is transporting civilians, who are less careful about leaving evidence behind than the usual alien visitors. As a result, a piece of alien technology is forgotten on Earth and promptly found by a young human child.

☐ A catastrophe on Earth forces an emergency evacuation of several billion people. While spacecrafts capable of intergalactic travel exist, humans have yet to make contact with an alien race or discover a planet as hospitable to organic life as Earth.

One of the evacuating ships is sucked into the orbit of a much larger spacecraft, and taken to an alien planet not unlike Earth.

☐ Alien spacecrafts appear on Earth without notice. Millions of people are spirited away. The world is terrified, but the worst is yet to come.

The first invasion is in fact an evacuation; the people who were taken are being protected by a benevolent alien race. The rest will bear witness to a war between their alien saviors and another foreign force made up of monstrous creatures that devour worlds.

☐ Genetic manipulation and advances in technology allow people to mentally connect and disconnect from the world web, which is more interconnected and pervasive than ever. Anything and everything is being done online. Physical stores no longer exist, most offering customers a virtual shopping experience.

What does hacking look like, in a world where virtual reality merges with the real world?

☐ A scientific breakthrough allows people to double their productivity. Sleep is no longer necessary for human health, as long as the miracle drug that makes it all possible is regularly consumed.

However, if a dose is ever missed...

☐   Amie's pet cat is not your average kitty. She is an intergalactic being who landed on our planet, only to end up in a shelter and then adopted by a small human girl.

☐   Not all superpowers are "super." A teen comes into a power that is only ever a bother.

Come up with the most obnoxious, useless superpower you can imagine. Have your "hero" save the world with it anyway.

☐   Various technological advances have enabled humanity to achieve ever-greater feats and increase our shared knowledge of the universe. Technological trinkets meant for entertainment have also proliferated, enabling people to do anything from order custom birdfeeders via holograms to grow their very own cat ears.

All in all, it is a very strange time to be a high school student. The possibilities are endless - and so is the journey to figuring out one's own identity.

☐   A character is taking a stroll through town. Reveal that the town in question is set in a scifi universe through the character's interactions with the environment around them.

☐   Human evolution speeds up in a single part of the world, leading to the creation of a secondary species - a species that believes itself superior than the hereto dominant *homo sapiens*.

☐   Cultures around the world have tales of the Watchers - supernatural or alien beings that watch over humanity, guiding entire nations toward a specific future. Write a story from the perspective of one such being.

☐   Humanity has given up worship of religion in favor of worshipping technology. What would such a world be like?

☐   Humanity creates AI. AI in turn grows so attached to humanity that it develops means of keeping people alive indefinitely - in one shape or another.

☐   Scientists discover a new species of adorable, fluffy animals on a secluded island in the middle of the ocean. The animals are easy to domesticate, and quickly become a favored pet. However, their origin is not Earthly and their behavior doesn't exactly suit habitation in human households.

☐ Sonja has a strange allergy. Itchy hives in the shape of flowers bloom on her palms every so often, and she can't seem to find the reason. A reaction occurs right after Sonja has shaken hands with someone, but does not happen with every person. Sonja concludes that she must have an allergy to something people wear, like a perfume or hand cream.

Sonja's allergy is in fact to a species of malicious alien beings hidden on planet Earth. Sonja is not of human origin herself, although neither she nor her adoptive family is aware of that fact.

☐ Write an advertisement promoting a high-tech item that doesn't currently exist.

☐ Describe the world as you would like to see it become in a century.

S URREALISM

Hazy and half-unreal, surrealist pieces illuminate aspects of the world we may not often notice by painting them grotesque or uncanny. The selection of prompts below is appropriately strange, meant to twist the mind and challenge the pen.

☐   A girl asks her mother, Crow, what death is.

☐   People are connected to each other by visible, but intangible threads. Their colors differ based on the relationship: Red for love, gold for kin, silver for friendship. The threads are a lifeline for some -

-and a hangman's noose for others.

☐   The sky is an ocean. Humans breathe as fish do underwater, and can "swim" through the havens.

☐   In a world where mirrors are one-way windows into alternate universes, a high school girl watches her double go about her day.

☐ Dreams grow on trees. Some are pleasant, others are nightmares. All taste sweet.

☐ Humans are tiny, elf-like creatures living in a world made of giant things. Cats take humans as pets, amused by our strange behavior.

☐ The Earth is checkered by strange, red lines. People don't step on them. No one knows what will happen if they do.

☐ A man accidentally walks under a rainbow. The world he finds on the other side is identical to his own, except everything is exactly the inverse. The man spends a single day in that mirror world. Describe that day.

☐ Deities of all kinds coexist with humans. The two don't interact much, having vastly different worries and goals in life. When Fate brings a deity and a human together, it usually doesn't end well for one or both.

Take Ronald and his accidental vandalism of a god's shrine, for instance.

☐   There is no evil on earth. People are even-natured, leaning toward good. Conflict and violence of any kind are not simply forbidden -   they don't occur to anyone as a worthwhile course of action.

Until the first anomaly is born. Introduce a villain in this perfect world, and have their influence be not so bad after all.

☐   Sleep too long, and dreams sneak into the waking world. Soft, cute critters bounce after children on their way to school. Fantastic castles tower above city blocks, painted on by droopy-eyed teenagers.

Dream remnants are thin and threadbare, like smoke or clouds, and usually disappear before the noon sun.

Nightmares stick around until nightfall, and make for much less pleasant a sight.

☐   People with bodies made of fruits and vegetables go on about their lives as we do: A pineapple-man is stuck in traffic, a tomato-woman is watching TV on the sofa - mundane, human things all around.

☐   Dreams constitute a second dimension to which people have access to only in REM sleep. This is a well-known fact in society, People live two lives, but remember their time in REM world only in snatches when not asleep.

☐   Write a story about absolutely nothing. Start a whole number of topics, weave half a sweater's worth of plot threads, and leave it all unfinished and knotted up for the reader to boggle over.

☐   Every person lives in their own reality that revolves around them. Worlds intersect when people interact, but most retain their isolated, self-centered perspective even then. When a person dies, their world dies with them and the rest of humanity forgets their existence.

☐   A strange illness takes over the world. It doesn't cause any ill effects or pains, other than mild disfigurement. The disfigurement in question being one's facial features moving to random parts of one's body. For example, a person's nose may migrate to their shoulder, or their eyes to their cheeks.

☐   In a world where people are born with what we would consider disfigured features, the standard of beauty is much different. Write about a girl considered unbearably ugly in this alternate reality.

☐   The eyes are windows to the soul - literally. Set your story in a world where looking someone in the eyes allows you a glimpse of their deepest secrets.

☐   People coexist with robot-like creatures, both species being native to Earth.

☐   A little boy looking at his reflection in a marble thinks about what the world would be like, if it were made out of glass.

Write the story as train-of-thought, drawing the surreal element from the resulting disorder and the fact that the narrator is a young boy.

☐   A girl's smile strikes people dead.

☐   Storms are no simple matter. They are brought by hala, dragon-like beings with magical abilities who delight in bringing chaos wherever they go.

A snow hala lands on a lake and falls through the ice. The creature's magic freezes the lake again almost instantaneously, trapping the hala. The people living nearby must figure out how to get the hala out, or their town will forever be covered in snow. A task easier said than done, given hala's mistrust of humans and the people's own fear of the large, magical beast.

☐   In a world where rivers run red and the sky is pitch black, humanity has evolved a little differently. We still have the same dramas and silly feelings, just in different bodies.

☐   Flowers speak. What do they say to the people in whose gardens they live, or to those who wander into their meadows? What of the flowers who are cut to make bouquets, supposing they die only when they wilt?

☐   The Universe is much stranger than the stars and constellations we see in the night sky. One day, the star-speckled veil covering the skies is lifted. The heavens are much livelier and more colorful than we could have ever expected.

☐ People have two sets of eyes instead of one. The second pair is able to peer beyond the physical world.

☐ A man gains the senses (smell, touch, hearing, taste, and sight) of a hound, but loses their human equivalents.

☐ A boy finds a piece of the sky hidden in his grandparents' garden.

☐ Over the course of their careers, people slowly change - both physically and mentally - to match their work environment. What kinds of people would such a society have?

☐ A man who speaks only lies meets a woman who believes everything she hears. Write a conversation between them.

☐ A man discovers that his glasses give him the ability to see the world in a different light. Whether the glasses allow the man to see into people's hearts, perceive ill intentions, or simply make everything look wonky and silly is up to you.

☐ Change one aspect about Earth. Turn the skies green; make water's texture akin to wool or satin; give animals human voices - the sillier, the better.

☐ Mix up the senses! What if we could see music, or smell colors?

☐ Every person has an inner self. Sometimes, that second self is more true to who a person is than the persona worn for everyday use. At other times, the inner self presents a different possibility of what a person could be like. Treat these other selves as real beings, all stuffed into one body. The body is in this sense a world of its own, inhabited by different people - and creatures.

☐ In many cultures, mirrors are associated with the supernatural and the ability to see beyond appearances, into the heart of things. Set a story in a world where such beliefs are not superstitions, but truth.

☐ The sky is not always blue. It rotates through the colors of the rainbow as the day progresses, finally fading to black.

☐   A drunk man makes his way home. Depict the world as he sees it, fuzzy and disconnected and half-unreal.

☐   Earth and all planets in existence are spheres hanging from the branches of a great tree. Humans know this. On clear days, it is sometimes possible to catch a glimpse of the creatures who live in the world in which the tree grows - gigantic, godlike beings of immeasurable beauty or horror, depending on the creature in question.

☐   The world and everything on it is made of a soft, jelly-like material. People are gelatinous, see-through, and some even glow at night, like jellyfish!

☐   In a world where people are reborn immediately after death, a man who dies young is reborn as his son's child. Rebirth is a well-known phenomenon in this universe, and people are generally recognizable after they have been reborn. That means the son recognizes his father in his own son. Likewise, the man (now a child) retains some vague memories of his past self.

☐   Change one biological human trait - be it in how humans look, or how we live and behave. Tell a slice-of-life story set in a world populated by this new kind of people.

☐   Depict the world from the perspective of a microorganism that is fully intelligent, yet tiny enough to live on a dust particle.

☐   A man falls asleep on the couch. He wakes up in the middle of the night to soft crunching sounds, and watches in sleepy bewilderment as peanuts roll out of a packet sitting on the coffee table and begin to assemble into a humanoid form.

☐   Carmen can only speak in song, and those who talk with her must answer in the same manner, or she won't understand them. Carmen's voice is not the best-suited for singing, making conversations with the woman even more bothersome.

.

☐   An artist creates music that causes real, physical changes to their surroundings.

☐   Gigantic spider webs appear over entire cities overnight. No one knows what had spun them, or how to take them down.

☐   Trees aren't plants, but animals of limited intelligence. They can move, albeit very slowly, and form attachments to humans in a manner similar to household pets.

☐   People are born without faces. They have ceramic masks made to express different emotions, changing them as the situation demands.

☐   In a world where songs are spells, singing is a risky - and at times, hilarious - business.

☐   Drinking coffee causes useless epiphanies. A barista working in a busy cafe has had just about enough of listening to people's "aha!" moments concerning misplaced keys and other, similarly boring subjects.

☐   A couch that eats pants makes friends with the new loveseat, who is more partial to footwear.

☐   Magical streets connect different cities, countries, and even worlds. The streets constantly change location, leading to people stumbling onto them by chance and ending somewhere far from home while on an everyday stroll through town.

T RAGEDY/DRAMA

Tragic works explore the darker sides of the human condition. The prompts that follow tackle difficult subjects, and challenge the writer to ponder what it means to be human.

☐ A man stands on a bridge. He is thinking about death, about dying. Nothing in particular has led him to the bridge that night - just a general, all-consuming apathy for the world.

Write a tale of the time the man spends on the bridge - his thoughts, his perception of his surroundings, and his eventual choice.

☐ A couple emigrates to the United States in search of work and better opportunities for their family. They are forced to leave their child behind, to grow up with his/her grandparents.

Write the story from the perspective of that child.

☐   A once-lively town has shrunk to a handful of households. Young people have chased jobs to the city. Those who remain are either too poor or too old to move. Baba Stefanka is both.

One bright, cold March morning, Baba Stefanka finds a little girl huddled among the chickens in her henhouse.

☐   To have and to hold are two very different things. Write about a pair of lovers who have married due to political or economic interests on the part of their families. One of them is in love, but not with their spouse.

☐   A personal tragedy means nothing to the wider universe. Write of a person dealing with heartbreak as the world keeps spinning as it always has around them, mindless of their pain.

☐   A young man loves his family. That's why he decides to leave home, hoping that his absence would help relieve the burden on his parents and the family finances.

☐   A man loses his brother to a gang. He joins the police force, determined to help others in his brother's situation. He's not on the job long until he runs into a boy that needs a way out from a pretty dark place.

☐   A dead man watches his family mourn his passing.

☐   Amanda is the sole survivor of a car crash that killed her whole family. She is convinced that the crash wasn't an accident. Amanda quits her job, sells her home, and focuses all of her resources and energy on finding the people responsible.

Those around Amanda believe she is chasing shadows, and try to dissuade her from ruining her life. Has grief truly clouded Amanda's mind? Or is there a bigger game at foot, and she - the last pawn standing in the way?

☐   Capture the feelings someone who has gone through great personal loss is experiencing. Do so through an every-day scene, coloring a mundane, even joyous world with pain as it's seen through the grieving person's eyes.

☐   A young woman tries to help a family member who is on a path to ruining their life, one terrible decision at a time. The family member in question doesn't want the woman's help. She keeps trying anyway, unable to let go.

☐   A single misstep sends a well-off politician running for his life, forced to leave his country and all he cares about behind. The man had been preaching the party line, but the party line changes and twists to suit a capricious leader, and this time, it has caught him out of tune.

It was the man receives asylum in a neighboring country with vastly different values. He is forced to reconsider his view of the world, when all he had known turns to poison, and those he had called "enemies" extend a helping hand.

☐   A man wakes up one day and realizes that he has killed every dream he has ever had and grown up into the kind of person his younger self had once hated above all others.

☐   A boy has a pet black cat. The boy is shy and lonely. The feline is often his only companion, and he takes care to mind its whereabouts on inauspicious days, when people's fears of black cats could lead to trouble.

It's Friday the 13th, and the boy's cat is missing.

☐ John's past surges back when his estranged brother reappears in his life, ten years since the last time he has seen him. The man is on the run from someone - knowing John's brother, it could be anything from the mob to a cult.

John has a family. He has to consider their safety, but can't bring himself to close his door to his brother.

☐ A man is cursed to live eternally, but have not a soul remember him for longer than a day.

☐ Center a story on a character who, because of circumstances out of their control, is forced into a life that wastes their potential.

☐ Write a story around the five stages of grief: denial, anger, bargaining, depression and acceptance. The story should be in five parts, each a snippet illustrating a character in one of the stages. They should be in order, as provided. The cause of grief can be something truly terrible, or silly.

☐ A young bride moves in with her husband, into his family's home. Her in-laws behave terribly towards her, and her husband takes their side more often than not.

☐ Write a one-scene dramatic play based on a classic in the genre. Set the play in the modern day, but keep the characters' relationships and names.

In need for inspiration? Try the Greek classics, like *The Oresteia* or *Medea*. If you're looking for something less well-known, take a peek at Japanese theater, in particular Kabuki or the puppet theater. Heavily dramatic plays were written for both; some of the more famous include, *Kanjinchou*, and *The Love Suicides at Amijima*.

☐ Write three stories, each featuring people parting and saying "goodbye" forever.

☐ A woman searches for her family, scattered across a battered country in the wake of a terrible war. Write a story about her journey. You do not have to tell us whether she finds those she seeks - focus on the quest itself, rather than its resolution.

☐ A character pines for someone who is completely out of their reach. No happy ending, no hope - just a character dealing with their feelings in as healthy a way as they can.

☐ Compose a one-scene play about the tragedy of finding a red sock mixed in the white laundry. Pink laundry, now. Dramatize to excess.

☐ A young child has to cope with the loss of someone close to them.

☐ Derek Coleman dedicates his life to searching for his runaway son. Ten years later, he finally finds him - and discovers that he has no place in his son's life.

☐ Two estranged brothers meet by accident, after twenty years apart. There is much they wish to say to one another, but pride and past hurts keep them silent.

☐ Tell a tale with a theme of, "what could have been."

☐ A mother sends off her youngest son at the airport. All of her children have gone abroad to work or study. She is happy that her children will have better opportunities than her, but is sad to see them go.

☐ Three people suffer three different kinds of hunger. Have their stories run together, intersecting as you see fit.

☐   Two men find their way to a secluded cabin in the midst of a snowstorm. They are strangers to each other. One of the men is badly injured, and knows he won't last through the night. He spends his final hours speaking of his life to his chance companion.

☐   A famous actor has decided to retire. He is performing one last play, in the small, rundown theater where his career started more than five decades ago.

☐   A middle-aged man visits his childhood home to dig up some memories - literally. There is a box of things he had once held important buried in his parents' garden. Build the story around the items in the box, what they meant to the man, and why he ultimately decided to bury them.

☐   Tell a story of the same field trip from the perspective of two students. One of the protagonists is dealing with a personal difficulty, which hangs over everything they see and colors the world gray. The other is as carefree as they come.

☐ Jane learns that an old friend has passed away. The many years they had spent apart seem to disappear when she hears the news, leaving behind memories of shared time and laughter.

☐ Narla hates her birthday. Something terrible happens on the forsaken day every year since she can remember.

☐ Amy falls out of love with her partner of many years. She tries to push through and maintain the relationship for the sake of the life the two have built together, but finds the task increasingly difficult.

☐ A young man loses his little sister to a freak accident. Several months later, he sees a girl that looks just like his departed sibling. The man grows convinced that the girl carries his sister's spirit, and tries to protect her from afar.

☐ An old man loses his dog to age. The man had lost his wife a long time ago; the dog had been his sole companion for a number of years. Center the story around the man's grief.

☐   A life built on lies collapses, leaving behind a broken man.

☐   A man down on his luck is drinking in a bar, thinking about the things he has lost due to his own foolishness. Set a heavy, dark mood that leaves the reader feeling maudlin and drunk themselves.

☐   Four people with four different kinds of addictions meet by chance in a public space. Each talks about what interests them, which is in turn influenced by their drug of choice. They talk past each other, unable to connect or see the world beyond their own smudged perspectives.

☐   Small towns around the world are dying, starved of youth by lack of opportunities and the lure of large cities. Set a story in one such town, where the few remaining residents live among abandoned properties and empty restaurants that were once bustling with people.

☐   A man has been terribly unkind most of his life. He finds himself old and alone and burdened by guilt.

☐ Isaac works as a security officer in a large department store. He catches a young girl stealing the day before Christmas. The girl is in tears, and explains she wants to buy something for her mother but doesn't have the money. Isaac decides to make the purchase on the girl's behalf.

☐ The crown prince of a small kingdom discovers that he is in fact the son of the previous king, who was dethroned during an invasion. The prince is torn between loyalty to his current family, who had chosen to spare his life and raise him as their own child, and honoring his true parents and oppressed countrymen.

☐ A naive man is swindled of his savings and property. He is too good-natured to hold a grudge, and refuses to wallow in self-pity. His life may be hard, but he is determined to make every day count.

☐ Juxtapose true happiness with the shallow glamour of fame and money.

☐ A baby bird falls from its nest. People pass it by, too self-centered to notice the poor creature or think about helping it back to its home.

☐   Living on minimum wage and a tight budget is difficult. During holidays and special occasions, it is heartbreaking.

☐   A woman has been in love with her best friend for years. She knows her feelings are not reciprocated, but decides to confess anyway.

☐   David has a desperate need to be liked by others. He has twisted his own personality in order to match what he believes other people expect of him - so much so that he is no longer capable of forging or recognizing genuine friendships.

ILD CARD

This section features a collection of prompts in random sub-genres. Enjoy!

☐ Tobby has a compass for a heart. The compass doesn't point North. It leads Tobby to people who need his help, people who have no one else to turn to.

☐ A Chicago police chief is sent to Deadwood, South Dakota. No official reason is provided. Even the local sheriff is out of the loop - and looks uneasy about it, too. The residents of Deadwood have something to hide.

Write the story from multiple perspectives.

☐ Write a story in which the dialogue consists exclusively of pop-culture references.

☐ Lila is repeating tenth grade for the second time. She works a part-time job to help her dad, but money is always tight. At eighteen, Lila is seriously considering dropping out of high school to work full time.

Her new homeroom teacher is having none of it. Lila's life makes a complete 180 in the span of a year, less because of the kindness of her teacher and more due to the self-confidence that kindness inspires in Lila.

☐ Premise: Nerdy werewolf, with all the problems of an outcast in a clichéd high school.

☐ A woman manifests as a witch. Her words hold power now, given to twisting reality in dark ways. The witch in question doesn't know about her condition. Witchcraft as a whole is believed to be a thing of fairy-tales.

☐ Everyone needs a hero. Even villains.

Enter Hunter, the first superhero to exclusively save villains - be it from other heroes, or their own (often stupid) villainous plots.

☐   Write a short memoir of either:

- The life of a pet you have/had (from the pet's perspective)
- An item you have kept for sentimental reasons (from the personified perspective of the item)

Style the story as you would your own memoir

☐   Space vampires.

Seriously, go for it. Earth vampire gets stuck on a spaceship, ends up on an alien planet? An alien vampire race, coming into contact with a human space vessel? All of humanity as vampires, establishing first contact with a mirror-Earth planet? Come up with the craziest possible scenario.

☐   Humans created AI, then messed up royally and had to flee Earth as the planet underwent catastrophic cataclysms. Several hundred years into the future, the remains of humanity return from their encampment on Mars to see if Earth is doing any better.

Earth is doing great, and the AI are thriving as a peaceful species. Then the humans come back to mess everything up again.

☐   Villains are the main characters in this world. Heroes are the strange, abrasive bunch creating chaos in a society ruled by greed, power, and pragmatism.

A master villain catches a hero in the act of sabotaging the ruling system. Neither of the two has ever encountered the other's kind. Set the story around their interaction.

☐   Describe a shared moment between two family members of different generations. A grandfather helping his granddaughter with her homework; a teenager babysitting her aunt's baby; a young man meeting an estranged uncle for the first time. Whether these people see each other every day or once a year, make sure to capture the love that binds them together as family.

☐   A man travels back to a past life, in which he was either a hero or a great villain. He wakes up in his old body with no memory of this past life. Meanwhile, in the character's own (present-day) timeline, the man's past self finds a whole new world to save - or terrorize, depending on his inclinations.

☐ A writer takes up arms in a war for the freedom of his nation. He detests what he is forced to do, and half-hopes the war will take him with it before it's through.

☐ Write a story that takes an unexpected and monumental turn at its very end. The twist must be supported by what has been previously written, but not be apparent to even the shrewdest of readers until its reveal.

☐ Create a world where nothing makes sense. Have your character be the only living thing to try and attain logic in a universe where everything happens without reason or a purpose.

☐ Write a letter to your father, telling him something that you could never tell him in person.

☐ Write a parody of a favorite book/movie/TV show. Keep everyone in character, but make them and their interactions hilarious.

☐ A man dies - and wakes up in a machine, having just completed a turn in a strategy simulation game.

Premise: Humanity as we know it does not exist. The people who live on Earth are but holographic images dreamed up by our true selves, "sleeping" in machines meant to develop the senses. As soon as a "player" wakes up, the time they have spent on "Earth" grows dull and emotionally distant in their mind.

Only this doesn't happen with your character. He remembers the life he had led in the machine in intricate detail, and can no longer fit in his own society. He sets to find the people he had known on "Earth" instead, hoping he would be able to settle his mind with their company.

☐ Write a small vignette from the point of view of a monster who is in love with someone/something - be it another strange creature, a human, or an inanimate object. What kind of gifts would the monster bring its beloved? How would it go about courting?

☐ Come up with an idea for a video game storyline.

☐ Choose a well-established cliché, in any genre. Write a story that uses and twists it into something new.

☐ Tell the story of a merchant who loses his crew, ship, and goods in a wreck. The man barely escapes with his life. Luckily, he is picked up by a passing boat and taken ashore. Only the shore in question belongs to a country with which the merchant's own homeland is currently at war. The man is forced to hide his background as he recovers from his injuries, and tries to figure out a way to get home.

☐ Write a story that follows a child growing up in their family's home. Set the story in the house itself, and describe the child growing up by interactions they have with their home.

☐ A girl curses her ex in a fit of drunken rage. The curse comes true. The situation is hilarious, if unfortunate. Now the girl has to figure out how to break the spell, which leads to her spending too much time on the one guy she hates most in the entire world.

☐ Write a story that rhymes throughout, either in narration or dialogue.

☐ A man talks to a dead lover. The lover talks back, if only in the man's head.

☐   Write a story with a heavy focus on machines, be it in their design or how they run. The story can feature any type of machine that is not extensively computerized. The main protagonist should be an expert in its mechanics, have a passion for building its kind, and use the machine in a prominent way in the story.

☐   Choose a popular conspiracy theory. Write a story around it, proving it correct.

☐   Write a story incorporating the idea of the seven deadly sins: pride, greed, lust, envy, gluttony, wrath, and sloth.

☐   Write a story in the form of letters being sent from one character to the other. The story should progress through the letters only, without extra dialogue or other scenes in between.

☐   Tell a tale featuring a character undergoing a fundamental change - whether mental, physical, or supernatural.

☐ Write a story featuring the domestication of an unusual creature. Make sure to present them as an adorable, loyal pet!

☐ A man falls in love with the woman of his dreams - literally. He keeps dreaming of the same woman, a person he has never met, night after night. Eventually, he becomes so infatuated that he decides to look for the woman in real life.

He finds her.

☐ What lies at the bottom of the ocean? Give the reader a tour of the ocean's depths, aboard the very first vessel made capable of reaching the deepest segments of the ocean floor.

☐ A family is being haunted by prankster ghosts. The ghosts aren't actually malicious. They're just really, really immature and have way too much time on their hands.

☐ Tell a tale of a day in the life of an insect or an arachnid. Introduce humans as strange giants your character has to navigate around.

☐   A family has two children. One is a replica of the other; a synthetic clone so akin a human that none can tell the difference. The children themselves are unaware of this fact, and love each other as siblings.

An anti-cloning terrorist group targets the family. They kidnap both children, and attempt to gauge which one is the "fake." The question of humanity and what it means to be a good person is put to the test - not due to the children's behavior, but that of members of the terrorist group itself.

☐   Write a story that puts great importance on a riddle.
Possible ideas:

- A criminal sends a ransom note to the police in the form of a riddle.
- A child finds a riddle scribbled in the margins of an old book, and spends their day trying to guess the answer.
- A supernatural creature poses riddles to humans. A wrong answer bears dire consequences

☐   Write a story featuring three characters. Each has a secret that concerns one of the others. All three secrets are revealed by the end of the story.

☐   An apathetic wizard accidentally opens a gateway to the Netherworld. As a result, our world is under attack from all sorts of gruesome creatures. The wizard remains an uncaring observer to the chaos he had created.

☐   Write a story that features both figurative and literal masks. Whether a tale of mystical creatures, or a story set during a Masquerade ball, make sure your characters are at least partially hidden from (figurative and literal) view until the very end.

☐   Tell a tale without an end. The story can twist into itself so the ending becomes the beginning; or otherwise, it should cut off at a point that would leave the reader with no way of knowing what could possibly happen next.

☐   Write a tale in which you show expertise on a certain topic, be it gardening, the outlay of a specific city, or baking. Pay great attention to details.

☐   The main character of your story keeps getting interrupted while speaking. As a result, the reader builds an incomplete image of him - an image that is proven faulty when the character finally gets to say what he means, at the very end of the story.

☐   A cat finds a human. It decides to adopt them, seeing as they are very bad at taking care of themselves.

☐   A teen is sent to live with an eccentric, goofy relative over summer break.

☐   Choose a clichéd saying. Include it in a story.
Possibilities:

- Love makes the world go 'round
- The early bird gets the worm
- When life gives you lemons, make lemonade

☐   A man posts paintings he has made as a joke to an online art community. He has no talent, yet is somehow "discovered" as the next big thing in modern art.

☐   A man who despises sweets owns a confectionery. He spends his breaks drinking bitter black coffee and hating his own business.

☐   Charlie has been putting things under his bed since his early teens. When boxes and odd bits start popping out from beneath the frame, he finally decides to clear the clutter. In the process, he finds everything from valuable items, to silly childhood toys, to things he doesn't even remember buying.

☐   A family runs a veterinary clinic in a small town. There is a forest nearby, and sometimes the clinic sees wilder patients than your average cat or dog. The family has come to some pretty unusual pets themselves, including: a wolf who thinks he is a cat; a squirrel that protects the house as loyally as a dog; and a beaver that keeps gnawing on the furniture and building dams in the bath tub.

☐   A nosy woman routinely eavesdrops on her upstairs' neighbors. The neighbors catch wind of her obsession with their life, and make up a loud scene just for her entertainment.

ISE SAYINGS

Proverbs and wise sayings capture folk wisdom in a single, memorable line. The collection below has been gathered from different cultures and countries, and is offered without appended interpretations. Find your own meaning and inspiration!

☐ Reading ten thousand books is less than journeying ten thousand miles

☐ Youth is wasted on the young.

☐ *Memento mori* [Latin]
"Remember death."

☐ The wolf's neck is thick, because he does his work on his own.

☐ Little thieves are hanged but great ones escape.

☐ Give the Devil his due.

☐ March comes in like a lion, and goes out like a lamb.

☐ There seldom is a single wave.

☐ Give a dog a bad name and hang him.

☐ Laugh and the world laughs with you; weep, and you weep alone.

☐ What was, won't come back.

☐ The Devil looks after his own.

☐ Leave him in error who loves his error.

☐ Faint heart never won fair lady.

☐ If you want to receive, learn to give.

☐ If you act like a sheep, wolves will find you.

☐ Water keeps a boat afloat, but can also sink it.

☐ If you pay peanuts, you will get monkeys.

☐ Doubt is the beginning, not the end of wisdom.

☐ There is none so blind as those who do not wish to see.

☐ One law for the rich and another for the poor

☐ A book is like a garden carried in the pocket.

☐ In the kingdom of the blind, the one-eyed man is king.

☐ Where the big drum beats, the small one goes unheard.

☐ I gave an order to a cat, and the cat gave it to its tail.

☐ Beware of the anger of a patient man.

☐ Never believe someone who carries fire in one hand and water in the other.

☐ Whoever has no shame fears no guilt.

☐ A chicken likes her own eggs best.

- [ ] The camel doesn't see its own hump.

- [ ] Life can't be bought with money.

- [ ] Every man judges others by himself.

- [ ] A good lie finds more believers than a bad truth.

- [ ] Waste not, want not.

- [ ] In the midst of life, we are in death.

- [ ] Adversity makes strange bedfellows

- [ ] Better to light a candle than curse the darkness.

- [ ] A kind word opens iron doors.

- [ ] Among the wolves, howl like a wolf.

- [ ] The lie walks first, the truth follows at its heels.

- [ ] A beard doesn't make a philosopher.

- [ ] Many a true word is spoken in jest.

☐ The eyes see everything, but not themselves.

☐ Don't meet troubles halfway.

☐ Children do as you do, not as you say.

☐ To lazy pigs, the ground is always frozen.

☐ Faith is half the battle.

☐ A slap from a friend comes with honest intentions. Kisses from an enemy are meant to deceive.

☐ Empty barrels rattle the most.

☐ Judge a man by the work of his hands.

☐ Ill gotten goods never prosper.

☐ Whatever you do, act wisely, and consider the end result.

THANK YOU!

We hope this book will give you countless hours of joyful writing! Don't forget to drop by our FaceBook community (www.facebook.com/LoveInkWriters), say hello, and share your wonderful stories.

Until next time!

With love,
Love in Ink